MAKING TIME, MAKING CHANGE

AVOIDING OVERLOAD IN COLLEGE TEACHING

Douglas Reimondo Robertson, Ph.D.

NEW FORUMS PRESS INC.

Stillwater, Okla., U.S.A.

NEW FORUMS PRESS INC.

Published in the United States of America
by New Forums Press, Inc.
1018 S. Lewis St.
Stillwater, OK 74074
www.newforums.com

Library of Congress Cataloging-in-Publication Data Pending

This book may be ordered in bulk quantities at discount from
New Forums Press, Inc., P.O. Box 876, Stillwater, OK 74076
[Federal I.D. No. 73 1123239]. Printed in the United States of
America.

International Standard Book Number: 1-58107-080-2

Cover design by Katherine Dollar.

DEDICATION

To my daughter

Maura Eileen Robertson

CONTENTS

ACKNOWLEDGEMENTS

First, I thank the hundreds of college faculty from around the country who participated in various overload workshops that I facilitated during the last two years. They shared their thoughts and experiences in conversations, in workshop discussions, and on index cards and reflection sheets that I asked them to submit. In important ways, they helped to shape the ideas that I present in this book, and I am grateful to them for their many significant contributions.

Next, I express sincere gratitude to the faculty, staff, and administration at Eastern Kentucky University for providing me with such a supportive and stimulating setting in which to think about college teaching. Eastern Kentucky University is truly an *engaged institution of opportunity* where largely first-generation college students work with dedicated and gifted teachers to develop not only as persons but also as citizens. Contributing to the public good and developing as persons are one at EKU—perfectly integrated, as they should be. I am proud to be associated with this merry band who do the good work far from the limelight. In particular, I extend special appreciation to Gail Hackworth in the Teaching and Learning Center, who helps me so immeasurably in my work as the center director.

Also providing me with a supportive and stimulating setting—in my whole life not just my work life—is my wife, Dr. Sue Robertson Reimondo, who has contributed in countless ways to this little book. I want to thank her for her transforming presence in my life—her quick intelligence, hearty good humor, endless energy, deep spirituality, appreciation of family, commitment to health in all ways, professional work ethic, stubborn desire to make the world a better place while having fun doing it, and most of all, her irrational love of me, something which I surely do not deserve and certainly have not earned, a kind of grace which she bestows upon me.

Finally, I should note that an earlier version of Chapter 8

appeared in the *Kentucky Journal on Excellence in College Teaching and Learning* (Robertson, 2003c), and has been revised for this book with permission.

ABOUT THE AUTHOR

Douglas Reimondo Robertson (Ph.D., Syracuse University, 1978) is Director of the Teaching and Learning Center and Professor of Geography and Educational Leadership at Eastern Kentucky University in Richmond, Kentucky. He has authored over 70 scholarly publications and presentations, including a well-received book on intentional change in adult life, which has entered its 3rd printing (*Self-Directed Growth*, 1988). Professor Robertson has helped to start three university faculty development centers (Portland State University, University of Nevada—Las Vegas, and Eastern Kentucky University), and has served as founding director at two of the centers (UNLV and EKU). He is the Senior Editor of the book series on college teaching published by New Forums Press. Recently, he was named to a four-year term as Editor of *To Improve the Academy* (two years as Associate Editor and two years as Editor). He sits on the Editorial Board of the *Journal on Excellence in College Teaching*, as well as providing frequent guest reviews for *Innovative Higher Education*. He is a founding member of the Editorial Board for a new electronic and print journal, *The Kentucky Journal on Excellence in College Teaching and Learning*. In addition, he has served on the Awards Committee for the Professional and Organizational Development (POD) Network in Higher Education and has chaired its Regional Organizations Sub-Committee. An active consultant since the 1970s, Dr. Robertson has provided over 110 trainings or consultations to a wide range of educational, health care, human service, governmental, and business organizations. Recently, he received a five year appointment as a Fulbright Senior Specialist and will be providing consultations for overseas universities through the J. William Fulbright Foreign Scholarship Board (FSB), Bureau of Education and Cultural Affairs of the Department of State (ECA), and the Council for International Exchange of Scholars (CIES).

CHAPTER 1

TOWARD DISMOUNTING THE DEAD HORSE

*"I will not be able to attend today's workshop (sorry—
I'm overloaded!!) but could really use some assistance
in this area."*

*"If you could just give me ONE of those [coping
strategies] RIGHT NOW, then I might be able to fit this
[workshop] in."*

"Sounds great. Can't come. Too overloaded!!!"

Faculty emails regarding a workshop
on coping with overload

Lack of time may be the single most commonly experi-
enced problem among American faculty. From my vantage as a
faculty development scholar and practitioner, I believe that it is
fair to say (although I could not prove it) that the overwhelming
majority of the roughly 400,000 full time faculty in American colleges and universities feel overloaded in their teaching lives; they
perceive that they do not have time to do their basic faculty duties
properly; and they believe that overload goes with the job.

We complain yet we do not reflect on and evaluate our
paradigms for how we use our time. Perhaps a pernicious norm
has evolved: anyone not complaining about being overwhelmed is
suspect. We act as if we have no choice.

Einstein once remarked, "Insanity is doing the same thing
over and over again and expecting different results." A Lakota
Sioux saying puts the idea in concrete terms, "When your horse is
dead, the proper strategy is to dismount." When it comes to avoiding overload, many of us sit on our dead horses kicking them in the
sides over and over again, insanely, wondering why we don't get
anywhere.

However, we do have choices about how we use our time. Einstein suggested a way to discover our choices when he further observed, "Problems cannot be solved at the same level of awareness that created them." Essentially, that is the objective of this book: to elevate our awareness of how we use our time and how we might improve that use of time.

We need to shift our perspective on using time from *subject* (a perspective *from which* we act naively) to *object* (a perspective *on which* we act intentionally). The tool that we will use to stimulate this shift in awareness comes from a vintage analysis of systems theory and research and focuses on managing the boundaries of our teaching selves better.

Avoiding Overload as Boundary Management

A little over 30 years ago, social psychologist Stanley Milgram attempted to explain fundamental differences in urban and rural living by exploring the ways in which individuals cope with information overload (Milgram, 1970). His argument was that city environments present individuals with much more information that demands their attention than they have attention to give. In these overloaded conditions, individuals necessarily adapt methods for controlling and limiting the amount of information that they have to process. The individual adaptations, when put together for whole urban populations, form an urban culture that differs from a rural culture where conditions of overload and related adaptations are much less common.

This line of thought helps to explain why when I moved to a small town recently and could not get the new wheel barrow in my car down at the hardware store, a total stranger without apparent hesitation put the wheel barrow in his pickup truck and hauled it several miles to my house. In the large city from which I had just moved, the good Samaritan would have stolen the wheel barrow.

Milgram's influential hypothesis generated much useful discussion and research among scholars who were attempting to understand the human experiencing of various kinds of environments, notwithstanding the fact that, as with much social science, the grand hypothesis was never definitively supported nor rejected. I began my professorial journey over a generation ago as a cultural geographer who followed closely the emerging discipline of environmental psychology and who was therefore familiar with Milgram's important hypothesis.

I could not help but think of this approach as I embraced the problem of helping faculty to "make time" in their teaching lives under conditions of overload. Metaphorically, perhaps colleges and universities are transforming from small villages to large cities. Some of them are certainly the size of cities when one adds together students, faculty, staff, and proximate business personnel.

Milgram extracted from systems science theory and research six ways in which systems typically adapt to conditions of information overload. I gave myself the assignment of restating these adaptations as principles that could be applied to college teaching in order to see if they had utility in helping faculty to manage better the boundaries that they set and the information flow that they allow in their relationships with learners. Then, I took these six principles into the world of teaching faculty to see if they worked.

Incidentally, for nearly ten years, I have pursued a line of work that has attempted to further conceptualize and professionalize the emerging role of the learner-centered college teacher (Robertson, 1996, 1997, 1999a, 1999b, 2000a, 2000b, 2001, 2001-2002, 2002, 2003a, 2003b). I have come to the firm conclusion that—whether we subscribe to learner-centered or teacher-centered models of college teaching—our management of the boundaries of teacher-student relationships is a vital element in the quality of the students' learning environment and our work environment. Yet little guidance is provided to teaching faculty regarding how to manage these boundaries effectively. That is why I focus on boundary management as a way to avoid overload. We need many more conversations regarding boundary management in college teaching, and this discussion of overload attempts to contribute usefully to these conversations.

I found two things from presenting my six principles in numerous faculty workshops in a wide variety of contexts. First, overwhelmingly, faculty found that the principles generated effective ideas for making time. Second, even if faculty were horrified by some of the ideas, these six principles tended to serve as useful *provocateurs* for stimulating faculty themselves to generate ways to make time that made sense for them. The bottom line was that the six principles consistently produced specific practices—either directly or indirectly—for faculty participants that made sense to them and that worked within their teaching lives.

Control/Flow Paradox

Typically embedded in a teaching professor's experience is a central paradox: we need to be in control, AND we need to go with the flow. "The test of a first-rate intelligence is the ability to hold two opposed ideas in the mind at the same time, and still retain the ability to function," observed F. Scott Fitzgerald (1945, p. 69). Being a professor requires this kind of intelligence.

On the control side, we become academics partly because of the promise of personal autonomy: being in control of our classrooms, our scholarly agenda, and our time. We are rewarded by our disciplines for being able to solve problems in a controlled manner. Even the word for our academic field—a discipline— denotes control. Being in control has value in a professor's life.

On the flow side, we discover that the key to success in academic work—doing something extraordinary in teaching, research, or service—involves being able to let go of control and knowing when to do so. For example, we cannot always control a learner's experience or a group's dynamic, and we need to recognize and give ourselves over to "teachable moments." Sometimes, we must submit to the "inner logic" of a scholarly problem in order to make progress with it. "Flow" symbolizes a force, energy, or essence that we can try to control and shape but sometimes (or perhaps, ultimately) to which we must submit. It is bigger than us—the answer to our research question; our classes' group dynamics; our departments', colleges', or committees' functioning.

Some faculty like going with the flow more than trying to exercise control, and for others, the reverse is true. Both are important. This book emphasizes ways to enhance control. However, the discussions occur within the context of this control/flow paradox and fully recognize the importance of flow. Actually, avoiding overload by exercising appropriate and effective boundary control helps to create the time and personal presence to be able to go with the flow when appropriate.

Background

Part of the foundation for this book is experiential—my own and other faculty's. For the last several years, I have been exploring how to avoid overload with faculty around the country in workshops and consultations. These faculty—who number literally in the hundreds—have provided valuable data and learning from their own work lives as well as important commentary on the validly of the ideas presented in this book.

Regarding my own experience, I taught my first college course in 1971, and I have been teaching in colleges in some way nearly ever since. For over 25 years, I have been working in some form of faculty development. I have helped to start three university faculty development centers and have served as the founding director at two of them. I have held the rank of full professor at three different universities, and I have been a faculty member at every major Carnegie type of four year institution—liberal arts, masters, and doctorate-granting. In addition, I have provided numerous consultations to faculty at community colleges. This experience of having been an overloaded college teacher while trying to advance through the professorial ranks and having helped other college teachers with the same struggle at a wide variety of institutional types plays importantly in generating and grounding this book's ideas and examples.

This book on overload is very much about the inner experience of being a college teacher. Therefore, also important in informing this book are the various scholarly literatures that address this inner experience. I have carefully examined over 200 books, monographs, chapters, and journal articles that provide either first-person accounts or researcher analyses of teaching professors' lived experience. Some book-length accounts with authentic and deeply disclosing autobiographical material on the teaching professor's inner life that I think are particularly useful include work by Brookfield (1990, 1995), Murphy (1993), Parker (1998), Tobin (1993), and Tompkins (1996). Of course, no single voice exists for the college professor, and I have actively sought the perspectives of traditionally marginalized or excluded perspectives, such as the following: (a) women professors, in general (e.g., Aisenberg & Harrington, 1988; Bannerji, Carty, Dehli, Heald, & McKenna, 1992; The Chilly Collective, 1995; Clark & Corcoran, 1986; Deats & Lenker, 1994; Ellsworth, 1989; Hayes, 1989; Heinrich, 1991, 1995; Heinrich, Rogers, Haley, & Taylor, 1997; Lather, 1991; Lewis, 1993; McElrath, 1992; Middleton, 1993; Rose, 1985); (b) African American, women professors (e.g., Carty, 1992; hooks, 1989; James & Farmer, 1993); (c) mixed race, women professors (e.g., Two Trees, 1993a, 1993b); (d) Native American, women professors (e.g., Monture-OKanee, 1995a, 1995b); (e) African American professors, in general (e.g., Jackson, 1991; Mickelson & Oliver, 1991); (f) African and Hispanic American professors, in general (e.g., Washington & Harvey, 1989); (g) Asian Pacific American professors, in general (e.g., Nakanishi, 1993); (h) Hispanic American professors, in general (e.g., Garza, 1993; de la Luz Reyes & Halcon, 1991; Padilla & Chavez, 1995); (i) Native American professors, in general (e.g., Cross, 1991); (j) women and minorities, in general (e.g., Boice, 1993a, 1993b; Bronstein, 1993; Bronstein, Rothblum, & Solomon, 1993; Johnsrud, 1993; Olsen, 1991; Tack & Patitu, 1992; Turner & Thompson, 1993); (k) working class, women professors (e.g., Tokarczyk & Fay, 1993); (l) working class professors, in general (e.g., Ryan & Sackrey, 1984); (m) lesbian, gay, and bisexual professors (e.g., Tierney & Rhoads, 1993); (n) critical professors (e.g., Shor, 1980, 1987, 1992; Shor & Freire, 1987); and (o) adjunct professors (e.g., Gappa & Leslie, 1993; Minahan, 1993). Furthermore, I have intentionally searched for accounts of the inner experience of college teachers in a broad array of institutional contexts: (a) community colleges (e.g., Baker, Roueche, & Gillett-Karam, 1990), (b) liberal arts colleges (e.g., Baldwin & Blackburn, 1981; Finkel & Arney, 1995; Tierney, 1991; Wright &

Burden, 1986), (c) masters colleges (e.g., Boice, 1992; Murphy, 1993; Ralph, 1978; Tierney, 1991), and (d) doctorate granting universities (e.g., Axelrod, 1973; Bannerji et al., 1992; Boice, 1992; Braskamp, Fowler, & Ory, 1984; The Chilly Collective, 1995; Mann et al., 1970; Minahan, 1993; Olsen, 1991; Olsen & Sorcinelli, 1992; Ralph, 1978; Whitt, 1991). I make no claim that this literature review exhaustively represents all of the perspectives of the American teaching faculty. However, I have energetically tried to include as many as possible and in so doing have included a good many. This book is intended to be a practical guide which is grounded in part in available scholarship but which emphasizes the readers' applications and problem-solving. As we go about exploring concretely your own development, after this brief description of scholarly foundations, explicit references will be rare. The merit of the ideas that follow will be their utility for you.

Intended Audiences

Notwithstanding the broad relevance of these ideas, I intend for this book to contribute to the quality of the working lives of teaching professors, regardless of their discipline or institutional type. Ultimately, I believe that students and student learning benefit from a faculty freed from overload. However, my immediate audience in this book is intended to be the students' teachers. The book's examples and contexts focus explicitly on college teaching and are set primarily in American colleges and universities. Also, the book should be of use for chairs, deans, and provosts who administer curriculum and instruction in higher education as well as faculty development professionals who administer and provide support services for teaching faculty.

Objectives

Two objectives inform this book: to generate specific practices that help teaching professors to avoid feeling overloaded, and to help teaching professors to create specific strategies for integrating these new behaviors into their daily practice (moving beyond simply recognizing what we should do, to actually doing it on a regular basis).

Overview

The book has two parts which correspond to the book's two fundamental objectives. Part I, Making Time, comprises six chapters and presents the six principles, one for each chapter, along with commentary and examples of how each principle would look when applied in our teaching lives. I encourage you to use the discussion of these six principles to heighten your awareness of how you use your time as well as to generate concrete ideas of how you might better use your time. Part II, Making Change, constitutes two chapters that examine how to integrate these changes into your practice by exploring change dynamics in yourself and in your environment. This discussion on making change adds significant new material to my previous book on intentional change, *Self-Directed Growth* (Robertson, 1988).

Charles Buxton wisely observed, "You never find time for anything. You must make it." The discussions in Part I are about "making time," a professor's necessary alchemy in this age of increasing expectations and decreasing budgets. A book on making time and avoiding overload probably ought to be short and to the point. So let's get started.

PART I

MAKING TIME

The six principles presented in Chapters 2 through 7, are in no particular order of significance, nor are they presented in a necessary sequence. Please feel free to examine them in any order that you want. They are freestanding but interconnected discussions which are structured more like a crystal lattice than a set of stairs.

As you read these six principles and how they might look when applied to the teaching life, think of things that you do to "make time," and perhaps make a list as you read. The concern of this book is not stress reduction or what you do to re-group, re-set, re-center, renew, or rejuvenate, when you feel overloaded. Although relieving stress is important, the focus of this book is avoiding feeling overloaded in the first place, particularly by managing the boundaries of your teaching role. This book tries to help us to structure our teaching lives so that feeling overloaded and stressed-out is a rare or occasional event rather than routine. Experiencing overload and complaining about it chronically should NOT be a norm in professional life and an indicator of a hard-working, dedicated professional.

Remember as you read these chapters that the purpose of managing the boundaries of our teaching selves better is to create time and energy for the really important (as we each define important) work of our teaching lives. It is not a selfish act but rather a professional responsibility. Being intentional about how we use our time increases our ability to be fully present and attentive when we need to be, rather than frazzled, exhausted, distracted, and late.

A central aspect of the teaching life is a press to take its many opposing demands—such as to be present and to restrict access—and to develop "generative paradoxes" (Robertson, 2003a, 2003b), solutions where both sides of opposing demands are satisfied in ways that create important synergies between them. For example, shifting responsibility from the teacher to the students to provide feedback to each other on their learning (Chapter 4) not only makes times for the teacher but also provides a potentially powerful developmental assignment for students.

Use the following discussion as a means of stimulating reflection on your conception of time and your approach to using time. Look for solutions to making time that benefit both you and the students wherever possible.

CHAPTER 2

BE ABLE TO BE EFFICIENT IN ALL THINGS

Related overload adaptation: "...allocation of less time to each input" (Milgram, 1970, p. 1462).

One way to deal with overload is simply to give less time to each demand. If we do this without dramatically reducing the quality of our response, we need to be able to do each task more quickly with the same or similar results. The formula could not be more straightforward. Same output + less time = demand for speed. This adaptation presses us to figure out ways that we can accomplish each aspect of our teaching more efficiently. The focus in this principle is on us. The notion of offloading or shifting the responsibility for some of our tasks to someone else comes later. Right now we look at being able to do what we do FASTER.

Notice that the principle advises us *to be able* to be efficient in all things. Having this ability does not mean that we need to be in our "efficiency mode" all the time. However, we do need to HAVE an "efficiency mode." Being a one-trick pony—having our own little, one way of doing things—just doesn't work anymore, if it ever did at all. We need a "control mode" and a "flow mode."

Also, please note that I am not advocating increasing our output as we increase our speed. We are not increasing our efficiency so that we can forever ratchet up the amount of work that we do. Chasing that pot of gold is patently unhealthy, and my intent is just the reverse—i.e., to help us to make our teaching lives healthier. To repeat, overload as a professional norm is pernicious. My argument is that in current working conditions many of us need an efficiency mode in order to cope in a sane way with our workloads, not to increase them so that we are still overloaded but merely producing more.

If you have a tendency to come down on the go-with-the-flow side of the professor's control/flow paradox, your defenses may be sky-high with this talk of speed and efficiency. "Don't just do something, stand there," you may be thinking. Rushing—like desire, in Buddhism—may be the source of all suffering, in your perspective. Serendipity, appreciation, creativity, simply thinking, all of these valuable human experiences may suffer under the hubris of control and the frenetic pace encouraged by honing efficiency, in your view. Rather than an efficiency expert, your may be an efficiency dunce, on purpose—an efficiency saboteur—because you deeply resist it. We will address this kind of resistance in Chapter 8. For now, just try to be as aware as possible of any biases you may have on the topic of efficiency and teaching.

Some of us are ingenious efficiency experts already, but no matter how efficient we are, we can always improve. Will Rogers wise-cracked, "You can be on the right track, but if you don't keep moving, you'll get run over." As you read the following examples, take what works for you and discard the rest. Please feel free to create your own applications as we go along.

Teaching Applications

Know Your "Lines in the Sand" and State Them Clearly, Early, and Often

Teaching professors are creators and administrators of educational policy, whether we like it or not. All of us have "lines in the sand" about which we feel strongly and are unlikely to compromise. As we teach and notice these things, we should articulate them as course policy statements which we communicate to the students clearly, early, and often, preferably in the syllabus but if not codified in writing then declaimed frequently in person. This practice not only makes sense in terms of sound evaluation practice—making expectations overt and specific for students—but also, it contributes to a surprising degree to our teaching efficiency. Not only do we save time by not agonizing over and over about what to do when students do something that we simply cannot abide, but also, we save time by not having to explain to individual students why we graded their work the way that we did.

These "lines in the sand" may sometimes be embarrassing to admit, at least some have been for me. For example, over the years I have found that I simply cannot with much confidence evaluate a five page paper which is submitted in response to an assignment that has a "suggested length" of ten pages, no matter how brilliant it is. Even worse is what to do about an eight page paper. No matter how good the eight page paper is, I am uncomfortable giving the paper the same points as an equally good paper that meets the "suggested length." I resisted it, but I finally had to admit it. Size mattered to me. I was a quality AND quantity kind of guy. So a number of years ago I formulated a policy about length, and I have been quite pleased with how it has simplified and improved life for both me and my students. I changed the phrase on all of my written assignments from "suggested length" to "minimum length." I explain to students early and often in writing and in person that responses that are less than the minimum length will have points deducted mechanically in direct correspondence with their shortness. If a minimum ten page paper is worth 100 points, then a nine page response can receive no more than 90 points, no matter what its quality. They may choose to write the paper as long as they wish. They will receive no extra points or consideration for writing well over the minimum length, but they will not be penalized. For some reason, long papers do not trouble me; however, I could see that for other professors it might. Those professors would have a different policy than mine, which is fine just as long as it is stated clearly and overtly to the students and to ourselves. In most courses, a student or a few students will find my policy annoying and me anal and will say so on the various feedback tools that I employ. However, the overwhelming majority finds the policy fair and appreciates its clarity. I cannot tell you the amount of time that it has saved. Anything that takes its toll on you in terms of your time and energy, no matter how profound or trivial, that relates legitimately to student behavior and the quality of the course experience—e.g., cell phones, pagers, side-talking, eating, tardiness, preparation, participation, civility, group work, and so forth—can often be handled more efficiently with a clear policy statement on your part that you share with students clearly, early, and often.

Interact with Students with Intentional Time and Depth

Set informal limits to interacting with individual students that are consistent with the amount of time and number of students that you have. Most of us have a comfortable rhythm for interacting with students—fast or slow, or somewhere in between—and we do not adjust it according to our class size. I am suggesting that if we try to give each course approximately the same amount of time—a reasonable general ambition—then a small class requires a different teacher interaction pattern than does a large class. This notion is not rocket science: the same time divided by lots of students or by just a few students produces less or more time per student. We need to adjust our interaction pattern accordingly. As with many of these recommendations, explaining this dynamic to the students (negotiating with others) as well as explicitly changing our interaction expectations of ourselves (negotiating with ourselves) helps us to change our behavior successfully and productively.

Use Technological Tools in Course-Related Scholarship

Perhaps the most fundamental demand of college teaching is content expertise. Content competence is a *sine qua non* of our relationship with our students. Professors, students, and subjects constitute a basic trinity of college teaching. We are supposed to know our subjects well and help students to learn those subjects.

Helping students to learn our subjects, of course, is usually a different matter altogether from our own, ongoing content mastery. Good teaching includes a commitment to developing effective teaching techniques, strategies, and materials. Along with our disciplinary subjects, many of us rightly include on our teaching-related scholarly agenda the topics of the learning process and facilitating it better for our normally diverse array of students.

Therefore, for both teaching-related content and process, we need to learn—and use—efficient ways to search and gather pertinent information, materials, and activities related to our courses. Whether we are keeping up with our existing courses or preparing new courses, we need to exercise our scholarly training routinely to gather knowledge efficiently.

Technological tools can help dramatically in this regard. For example, Internet search engines explore web-based data sets quickly and effectively and can make tremendous amounts of time for teachers to use in other ways. When needing quickly to update ourselves on a topic, we can employ any number of web-based search tools which rapidly deliver to us abstracts of much of the latest published work on a particular subject. The advanced search options in these tools allow us to exercise a remarkable degree of precision in these searches.

Web sites regarding teaching of our subjects may exist with collections of instructional units. With the advent of the scholarship of teaching and learning movement, some of these web sites are even peer reviewed, as the effort develops to support the promotion, tenure, and merit reward of professors' scholarly commitment to teaching (e.g., http://www.merlot.org).

When selecting texts, why spend time choosing a book only to discover that it is no longer in print? Instead, we can conduct searches of web data bases that function like user-friendly versions of the old, mammoth, hard-copy *Books in Print*. We can electronically search these data bases of books in print much like we would search a library or any literature data base. Some sites include editorial reviews (e.g. http://www.amazon.com).

When looking for good visuals for handouts, overheads, PowerPoint, or web pages, teachers can use search engines to locate photos, illustrations, and figures, which then can be copied by using the right mouse click menu and saving as a .jpg file (unless protected). These examples are just the tip of the iceberg.

We can employ two age-old and potentially inter-related strategies in identifying and using web sites: (a) *hunting and gathering*, and (b) *cultivating and harvesting*. In hunting and gather-

ing, we use a search engine such as Google (http://
www.google.com) to hunt, then we gather. Simple, really. But
also time consuming. When we add the bookmark and folder tools,
we create the cultivating and harvesting option, which I highly recommend. We can create e-files of web sites related to our particular teaching interests. As we are going about our occasional hunting and gathering, or just going about our daily business (reading
the resource exchanges on the various email lists to which we be-
long, or reviewing the teaching section on the e-Chronicle for example), we are always looking to add a good site to our teaching
file. We are cultivating those files. Then, when we want material,
rather than hunting and gathering, we go to those files and harvest
material from the web sites. If we have cultivated these files well,
the harvest is abundant.

Thinking of colleagues who are aware of these tools and applications is easy. However, identifying colleagues who use them
regularly is often difficult. For this reason, I began this section by
emphasizing that we not only need to learn efficient methods for
gathering course-related information, but we need to use them. We
need to integrate them into our regular practice.

Use Technological Tools to Check for Plagiarism

When suspecting a student of plagiarism, professors can
break a sweat in the library trying to find the smoking gun. However, professors no longer have to rifle through hundreds of books
themselves thinking, "I know that I have seen this passage somewhere; now where did I see it?" or "This student does not write
like this; what is a likely source for this voice?" Estimates of the
degree to which college and university students plagiarize or buy
papers on the Internet are staggeringly high. However, the same
technology that helps students to plagiarize can help teachers to
confirm it. Teachers can simply enter suspect sentences in the
Google search engine (http://www.google.com). Often, it will find
the original sources for us within seconds. A cottage industry based
on selling term papers has quickly turned into big, web-based business. However, the market has bred web-based detection services
in response. The jury is out on whether or not these services are

worth the price. If you and your colleagues are spending large amounts of time on these particular issues of academic integrity, you may want to investigate these services. Meanwhile, good, old Google is always there, and free.

Use Robots to Score and Record Tests

Another teaching task that can take a lot of time is scoring and recording student performance on multiple-choice tests and quizzes, if you use these kinds of evaluation tools. Course management systems such as Blackboard and WebCT have tools that do this work for us. As with the previous set of ideas, we should let robots do the work wherever it makes sense. Although accessed via the web, these tests normally need to be proctored in order to control for cheating, which means that we need to give them in a supervised class setting where the students have computers with Internet access.

Digitize Everything That You Can

Teaching materials, such as photographs, illustrations, graphs, charts, maps, video clips, sound clips, textual excerpts, outlines, notes, and the like, can all be digitized and stored on electronic files. When converted to this digital form, through the use of various tools that are available to faculty in some way at most universities and colleges, these materials become much easier with which to work and creating effective presentations, handouts, web sites, and so forth, becomes much less time consuming. Furthermore, updating, elaborating, editing, reassembling, or changing these materials in any way is relatively easy when they are in digital form. The potential time savings that are created by digitizing instructional materials—not to mention the upgrade in the quality of those materials—begs us to figure out how to integrate this practice into our teaching lives.

Word Process Written Feedback

Providing students with written feedback is an important element of the instructional process. We need to try to set up submission systems that allow us to word process our feedback whenever possible—for example, electronic submission of Word files which we can save and on which we can comment for return to the students as email attachments. Even if student work is turned in as conventional hardcopy, we can still word process our feedback.

Why should we? Many faculty can type faster than they can write. Furthermore, students often cannot read faculty handwriting any better than faculty can read students' handwriting. We end up wasting our time providing feedback which the students cannot decipher and do not bother to have interpreted, or we waste it having to read our comments to students when they approach us after class wondering what it is we were trying to say in our illegible scrawl. In addition, the pressure on conscientious faculty to phrase handwritten feedback well the first time is eliminated if we can easily delete, re-phrase, and spell-, grammar-, and thesaurus-check our commentary with a word processing package. Finally, not infrequently, professors may have to give the same feedback over and over again to different students, and cutting and pasting commentary can save a lot of time.

Use Group Feedback Thoughtfully

Provide group feedback on student work where possible in lieu of feedback to individuals. For example, I often assign weekly reflection papers for required reading ("What stood out to you?"), an assignment that can generate a large number of papers requiring some kind of reading, evaluation, and feedback each week. Papers are graded pass (all the points) or try again (no points, but please re-submit). All apparently sincere efforts that meet the minimum length requirement receive a pass and all of the points. So much for the grading; other kinds of feedback present bigger challenges. I find that I simply cannot read and comment on each individual paper and keep up. So I began the practice of reading all of the papers and looking for themes among them. I give oral feedback to the group about these themes. A few papers might require written feedback, for example because of their sensitive, personal content. I need to explain my system to the students upfront (negotiate with others) as well as become convinced myself that I am not being lazy or irresponsible and that the reflection assignment still has considerable educational value with this form of feedback (negotiate with self).

Remember that Perfect Is Not Beautiful

My wife and I repeat this thought over and over when we paint a room in our house. It is our painting mantra. Actually, it is our home improvement mantra. Visitors think that the house looks wonderful, even though the paint job has a few minor and almost imperceptible imperfections. Perfect is not beautiful—the mantra works well in teaching, too. Perfectionism is grossly inefficient. I am a perfectionist in recovery, and I make this statement based on abundant personal experience as well as observations of colleagues during my 30 years of college teaching. Perfectionism sucks up our time and energy as we pursue a fantasy of perfect teaching performance well beyond the point of diminishing return. Furthermore, perfectionism can paralyze us. For example, we may let student work build up because we do not have time to give "proper" feedback. Many times, I have had 60 student reflection papers to read in a week and just enough time to read them but not enough time to comment on them. So I have put off returning them and committed myself to doubling up the next week. Then, I faced 120 papers with impossible expectations of myself and even less time. I felt overwhelmed. Feeling overwhelmed—like feeling lost, really lost (have you ever really been completely lost?)—can be terrifying and utterly depressing. I have learned that I need to cut my losses and keep up. Our expectations of what we can do must fit the realistic opportunity that we have to do it. Otherwise, we can become stuck and do little or nothing. Perfect is not beautiful.

Do Not Permit Handwritten Student Work

We need to develop a variety of reading speeds, including speed reading, for processing course materials and student work. Handwritten student work cannot be read easily at various speeds. Also, in this computer age, not requiring students to use word processors may do them a grave disservice. Of course, exceptions will always be necessary.

Parse Your Time and Set Appropriate Expectations

Be cognizant of the time available for the various aspects of the course—e.g., your class preparation, feedback on student work, faculty-student interaction—and try to set appropriate expectations in participants (in you and your students) from the beginning of the course. For example, we know that learners benefit from having feedback on their work. In fact, in terms of educational outcome, evaluating student work and providing feedback probably merits as much time as preparing good content. Our teaching load may only leave us an average of two hours per week for each of our courses to prepare for class and to evaluate student work. If we split that time equally between class preparation and evaluating student work, that would allow one hour per week per course to provide feedback on student work. One hour is not enough time to read and comment on 60 one-page reflection papers, to use a previous example. So I need to provide group feedback. However, I need to explain the reason that I am using the group feedback technique to students initially, and I need to repeat that explanation often. Otherwise, student motivation is doused because I have not responded personally to them, and they figure that it has something to do with them or their work. The next principle (Chapter 3) helps with this critical challenge of assigning times to tasks.

CHAPTER 3

EXPRESS YOUR VALUES IN HOW YOU USE YOUR TIME

Related overload adaptation: "...disregard of low priority inputs" (Milgram, 1970, p. 1462).
Corollary: "Principles of selectivity are formulated such that investment of time and energy are reserved for carefully defined inputs..." (Milgram, 1970, p. 1462).

Despite being in the latter stages of a terminal illness, my mother resisted making a will. She did not want to assign relative value to her relationships with her sons, grandchildren, sisters, brothers, nieces, nephews, and the rest of her rambunctious and endearing clan. The endeavor was overwhelming to her, which I certainly understand. She preferred to ignore the distribution of her modest estate, and let the court do it for her with rules that in her worldview had a "law-of-nature" status like gravity or the speed of light. It needing doing; she just didn't want to be the one to do it. Being a gentle lady from Texas, she did a graceful, little Texas two step around the whole issue.

I think that many of us exhibit this approach to managing our time. So many good things vie for our time that we have difficulty choosing among them. So we don't. The choice gets made— usually whatever comes at us "firstest with the mostest." We abdicate our authority to make the choice and let circumstances and our social environments do it for us.

At its most fundamental level, managing time intentionally is about consciously choosing between two (or many more) good things. It is about making difficult choices and committing ourselves to those choices. Most profoundly, using time intentionally is about values conflict, discernment, and commitment. Time is a resource: we must learn to invest our time in what we value— and to say "no"—in correspondence with our deepest priorities.

Teaching Applications

If we are going to give time to that which we value, then we have to discern what we value and explicitly allocate our time accordingly. The following process helps us to do this with regard to our teaching lives.

Identify the Major Areas of Your Life

Let's start big with the whole ball of wax: our whole lives as we are living them at this moment. I know that this book is specifically about the teaching life. However, to accomplish what we need to in this chapter, we must start with the whole and work back to this particular part.

Begin by answering these questions. To what do you give your time currently? How would you describe the major areas of your life, as you organize your life right now? For example, work would be one. Family might be another. Friends perhaps would constitute another. Maybe you have a hobby. Inventory your typical use of your time.

Answering the next question may generate a different set of responses than those that you just gave, and it may not. In your conception of a balanced, healthy life, how would you use your time? This question is not one of those if-you-won-the-lottery-what-would-you-do type questions. I am not asking you to fantasize here. Given your current finances, obligations, various constraints, and so forth, are there important activities missing from your life that you would like to add? For example, some of us declaim our spirituality as the most important part of our lives, yet some of us who say that spiritual development is important give it no time each day or week. Furthermore, our good health may be a part of our assumptive world; we may take it for granted. However, at some level we know that we need to cultivate and nurture good health, or it can go away. Yet we may give no time to exercise and eating well, and we may not give enough time to rest. In another example, our relationships with our children may be terrific; however, our marriages may have fallen into neglect. Many of us may not give any attention during each day or each week to building our relationship with our spouses.

One exercise that helps to discern the most important areas of your life—among the many—is to create an "absolute YES" list, which is limited to a specific number of items—say five. This list comprises things that you commit to giving time, no matter what. You commit to saying "yes" to them each day or week above the other activities that beg for your time. In the whirl of daily living, among all of the competitors for your time, attention, energy, and passion, these items have been chosen by you, in correspondence with your values, to be privileged. They can be anything, including "being spontaneous" or "stopping to appreciate the moment." Living intentionally does not mean living in robotic, rational slavishness to lists. It means living with the recognition that every moment presents us with a choice, that not making a choice is a choice nonetheless, and that we have the potential to influence significantly the quality of our lives and the lives of those around us through our choices, moment by moment.

A folksy algorithm tells us to look at what we do with our time, to discern toward what end we invest the use our abilities, and to examine our checkbooks and charge card summaries—in other words, identify how we use our time, talents, and treasures—then we will know what we really value in life, no matter what we say. When you focus on at least the time part of that equation, would you like to make any changes in the way you structure your life on a day by day basis?

This exploration of overload and managing time—if it is to be honest and substantive, rather than flip and gimmicky—gets down to this deep level of inner questioning quickly. Why not take this opportunity to commit to changes that bring your espoused values in closer correspondence with your lived values? If they already are, good for you.

Assign Times for Each Area

Among the entries in the canon of aphorisms about time are many sayings that use a money metaphor to communicate that time is valuable and that we should it wisely. For example:

Remember that time is money.
Benjamin Franklin

Minutes are worth more than money. Spend them wisely.
Thomas P. Murphy

*Time is the coin of your life. It is the only coin you have,
and only you can determine how it will be spent. Be
careful lest you let other people spend it for you.*
Carl Sandburg

*Time is a fixed income and, as with any income, the real
problem facing most of us is how to live successfully
within our daily allotment.*
Margaret B. Johnstone

Essentially, based on our values, we are creating a time budget here, similar to but different from a financial budget. In a financial budget, we all may have vastly different amounts of money to allocate. However, in a time budget, we all have the same bottom line: 24 hours in a day X 7 days in a week = 168 hours in a week. One hundred sixty eight hours a week—no more, no less— exists for each one of us. How do we want to use that valuable time?

A week may be an inappropriate budgeting frame for us. Perhaps we want to use a biweekly, monthly, or seasonal budget. For example, a professor's time budget may look differently during the summer than during the school year or when on sabbatical in contrast to normal residence. Or a professor's semester rhythms may require different weekly time budgets for the semester's beginning, middle, and end, as well as an adjusted intersession budget, all considered together in determining whether or not the budgets fit the professor's goals and objectives. Whatever frame makes the most sense for us is the one that we should use.

For the sake of illustration, we will settle on a weekly frame for our time budget. We need to assign a specific number of hours per week to the major areas of our lives that we have identified. This task usually requires some tough choices. Stick with it.

When the dust settles from this struggle, you should have determined the amount of time that you want to devote to your work in a balanced, healthy life. For example, let's say that we choose to dedicate an average of 50 hours per week to our work.

Of course, the number of hours per week that we devote to our faculty work may change during the course of our career. For example, the pre-tenure figure may be higher than the post-tenure figure because of the magnitude of what lies in the balance of the tenure decision.

Nonetheless, right now, for this moment in time, with full recognition that it may and probably will change, we need to commit to a particular number of hours—not substantially more nor less on average—that we are going to give to our work.

Identify the Major Areas of Your Faculty Work

Now we need to follow a similar procedure for our work life that we followed for our whole lives. To what do you give your time currently in your faculty work life? How would you describe the major areas of your faculty work, as you organize that work right now? For example, teaching would probably be one, with advising perhaps being a part of that teaching responsibility. Scholarship directed toward publication might be another major area of your faculty work. Participation on various faculty committees surely would constitute another. Inventory your typical use of your faculty work time.

In your conception of a balanced, healthy faculty work life, how would you use your time? Again, I am not asking you to fantasize in responding to this question. Given your current context—institutional type, discipline, stage of your career, salary demands, and so forth—are there important activities missing from your faculty work life that you would like to add? For example, many of us recognize that we need to continue to learn and develop throughout our careers and that this kind of professional development takes time. Yet many of us do not give it regular time. We would like to learn Blackboard or PowerPoint, but we do not have time. We would like to reflect regularly on our teaching experience in writing or with colleagues, say in a faculty learning community, but we do not give it time. We would like to read in areas that pertain to our work but are outside our discipline, but we

do not give it time. Another example might be our wish to cultivate relationships and community in our departments, colleges, and
universities. We would like to take advantage of lunch for this
kind of relationship-building, but we do not make the call or write
the email to make the date. Relationship-building takes time, but
many of us do not give it any regular time. Many possible commitments exist for faculty work. What is on your "absolute YES
list" for your work?

Assign a Weight to Each Area

Now create a time budget for your faculty work that as-
signs percentages (or weightings) to your top faculty priorities.
For example, let's say that our four major areas of faculty work
and their relative weightings (expressed as percentages) are as fol-
lows:
- Teaching and advising, 50%
- Research , 30%
- Service, 10%
- Professional development, 10%

Do the Math

Now we simply multiply our percentages (or weightings)
by the amount of time that we have allocated for our faculty work
per week. In our example, where we have budgeted 50 hours per
week for work, the results are as follows:
- Teaching and advising, 25 hours per week
- Research, 15 hours per week
- Service, 5 hours per week
- Professional development, 5 hours per week

Keep Doing the Math

Because this book is about teaching, we focus on that 25
hours per week that we assign to teaching. How many courses do
we have? How many courses are separate preparations? What are
the relative states of development of the courses, ranging from new
to well-developed? Are we trying a major innovation in one or

some of them? How many required office hours do we have each week?

If we subtract the number of office hours that are required each week from the 25 hours, then we have the amount of time that we have to divide among all of the courses in our teaching load. For purposes of illustration, let's say that we have a four course load, that we choose to commit an equal amount of time to each course, and that we have four office hours required of us each week. A summary of the distribution of our teaching time would appear as follows:

- 25 hours per week for teaching and advising
- Minus 4 office hours per week
- Leaves 21 hours per week for teaching to be divided by a 4-course load
- Which results in about 5 hours per week for each course
- Which means for each course, about 3 hours per week in class and about 2 hours per week for preparation and feedback on student work

Using this procedure, we have a true reading, which is based explicitly on our value system and is anchored in our whole life as we organize it at this moment, of how much time we have available for our teaching. We could productively follow a similar line of questioning that we have just pursued with regard to our whole lives and our work lives: *viz.*, how are we spending our teaching time, and how do we think that we should spend our teaching time?

Use Discretion in Disclosing the Details

"Happiness is a form of courage."
Holbrook Jackson

We need to negotiate with our environment—for example, with our students and with our colleagues—the expectations that they have of our role performance as teachers, just as we need to negotiate those expectations with ourselves. Disclosing the bottom line number of hours that we have available for a course may help in these negotiations with others. However, as a rule, I do not recommend revealing the details of the process through which we just went.

Most students do not understand all of the demands that are placed on professors. Often, they see professors—as many parents and legislators do—as only teachers. We could take on the added task of teaching them about the professor role in higher education—about the trinity of teaching, research, and service, or the Boyer framework of discovery, integration, application, and teaching. However, most of us are challenged enough by merely trying to teach them chemistry, history, literature, geography, or whatever our subject happens to be.

When it comes to our colleagues, most of whom want to be supportive of us and good citizens of the university, disclosing the details of our work life and time management is definitely not recommended. Except under extraordinary circumstances, I would keep private the number of hours that I budget for work per week, the major areas of my faculty work as I define that work, and the weightings that I give those various areas. I would share them only with a trusted few.

I make this recommendation with sadness but also with good reason. It seems that no matter how many hours per week that we work, someone always feels compelled to "one-up" us and shame us. If we say, "Forty," they say, "Fifty." If we say, "Fifty," they say, "Sixty." Their full reply may sound something like this, "Seventy hours a week! Is that all?!? I work at least 80, sometimes 90, and only need four hours of sleep a night." Given the highly political nature of most departments, colleges, and universities, and given the fact that peer perception of us matters importantly in promotion, tenure, merit, and other kinds of significant rewards, we understandably pay attention to these shamings and have trouble brushing them off.

A week comprises 168 hours. When asked how many hours a week I give to work, I reply preemptively, "One hundred and sixty eight." Unless the person is interested in a serious conversation about time, work, and values, or unless the person is genuinely suffering from stress and really needs someone to listen, I try to change the subject gracefully in order to avoid the posturing that often ensues when it comes to talking about how busy we all are. How can we be so busy and spend so much time telling each other how busy we are? Sometimes, these self-serving testimonials may have more to do with impression management than anything else. We need to appear busy to each other and to ourselves.

I am not sure how it happened, but I am afraid that a norm has developed in which insanity—or lack of health—and working to the point of being overtly and chronically stressed has become an indicator of a serious and dedicated professional. I reject that notion and strongly encourage others to do the same. Dealing with shaming responses to our healthy commitments is needlessly distracting and debilitating, and we can choose to avoid them. "Happiness is a form of courage," and we need to support that courage in each other.

CHAPTER 4

DON'T HOARD
RESPONSIBILITY, SHARE IT

*Related overload adaptation: "...boundaries are
redrawn in certain social transactions so that the
overloaded system can shift the burden to the other party
in the exchange" (Milgram, 1970, p. 1462).*

Essentially, this principle involves sharing course responsibilities with other agents rather than trying to do everything ourselves. Most likely, the educational outcomes—the student learning—will be even better when we spread around the responsibility and get more participants actively involved in the learning process than when our doing everything encourages passivity and dependence in students and impoverishes the learning environment by restricting the voices in it to one dominant one—our own. Enhancing the learning by sharing the responsibility—i.e., creating effective active learning—is really the challenge of applying this principle. If we are successful, students learn more, and we make time for ourselves. In other words, active learning—done well—can help students learn and teachers avoid overload.

As we will see in the following teaching applications, this principle challenges our need to control. Remember that control and flow seem to constitute a fundamental paradox for professors: both appear to be necessary to do exemplary teaching, research, and service. Even so, we may be inclined more toward one than the other. Some of us go with the flow more easily than others, while others of us feel more comfortable exerting control over situations than others. The idea of giving over responsibility to other participants to provide content, feedback, logistical support, and various other elements of instruction may precipitate in us a flurry (or perhaps even a blizzard) of feelings, such as guilt, shame, fear, anxiety, and so forth. As you review the possible teaching applications that follow, try to be aware of your emotional response to them. This awareness will come in handy later in Chapter 8, when we explore our resistance to change—even change to which we are strongly committed.

Teaching Applications

Employ NIFs

A NIF is some type of <u>N</u>on-teacher <u>I</u>nstructional <u>F</u>eedback—information from any source other than the teacher that students can use to understand the quality of their learning and, ideally, how to improve that quality. Students—like teachers or actually like any human beings—learn best when they use their learning and receive immediate and high quality feedback on their performance. Actually, the importance of providing learners with good feedback, quickly, is so great that it should probably receive equal attention from teachers as providing learners with good content.

Feedback does not necessarily mean giving a grade, although a grade is certainly a form of feedback. We are not talking about teachers abdicating their grading responsibility when we recommend sharing the responsibility to provide learners with feedback.

Providing feedback takes time, sometimes a lot of time. As teachers, we need to manage the feedback process. However, we do not need to be the sole source of feedback that students receive on their learning. We can use NIFs (non-teacher instructional feedback) to shift the task from ourselves to provide feedback to other entities. The task with using NIFs is to strategize explicitly to identify good sources of instructional feedback (that are NOT us) and to integrate them intentionally into our courses.

Explaining to students what we are doing, and why, has real value in terms of empowering their future self-directed learning projects as they deepen their understanding of the learning process—the importance of feedback and the many sources of feedback available to them. Discussing our rationale for using NIFs with students also tends to nip in the bud unfounded accusations from students that we are shirking our responsibilities and goofing off. Throughout this book, we see that negotiating with ourselves and negotiating with others provides good returns when we are trying to integrate new practice into our teaching. The following sections discuss four possible sources of NIFs.

Students. Often, students provide a good and abundant source of instructional feedback for each other. Student-to-student feedback might occur in short term, dyadic or small group exchanges in class, enduring work groups that may involve face-to-face meetings outside of class, or electronically mediated *agorae* such as distribution lists or discussion boards on course management systems such as Blackboard or WebCT.

For an example of an easy-to-use technique, recall my use of weekly reflection papers (Chapter 2). The value of these assigned written reflections in students' learning processes is something that over 25 years of my using them has taught me. However, they beg for feedback to realize their full learning potential. Providing that feedback is time consuming. Remember that as an efficiency I have had to resort to giving group feedback on these reflections by identifying themes that individual papers share and speaking to those themes at the ensuing class meeting. I do not comment in writing on any paper, except those that include particularly personal material and seem to require a response from me. I let students know this practice, and why, early and often in order to minimize the predictable and understandable disappointment they might feel when they receive their papers back from me with points on them but no comments. Negotiating our practices with self and with others usually increases their effectiveness and helps us to stick with them. Importantly, I do not merely provide this feedback from me; I enhance this teacher-generated group feedback by using students to give feedback to each other.

Here's how it works. Over the years, as students have reflected on the week's reading and written about what stood out to them about it, they have expressed curiosity about what other students were writing. So each week, when students' reflection papers were due, I began to give 10 minutes to having students pair up and explain to each other what they wrote about—what stood out to them. The payoff from the investment of so little time was remarkable.

In terms of feedback, students got it and gave it, both of which tended to deepen their understanding of the material and to develop them personally. "To teach is to learn twice," as the saying goes. In explaining their reflection papers, students were teaching each other, and both students tended to learn more than knew before they began the exchange. In responding, a press was on for students to enter into the worldview of this fellow student right in front of them and to try to understand vis-à-vis their own frame of reference, a process which encouraged critical thinking and cognitive development.

Also, this reflection sharing ritual created social pressure to come up with something interesting to share. A student remarked to me early in my use of this technique that she read differently knowing that she was going to write a reflection paper than she did when she was just reading to complete the assignment. This observation has been repeated over and over again to me by students. Knowing that they are not only going to have write a reflection paper which I will read but also to explain that paper to a student colleague reinforces student accountability and encourages sincere effort. Student-to-student feedback became a part of the course's motivational infrastructure as well as providing students useful feedback.

In addition, the procedure creates a considerable amount of energy in the classroom and functions like an effective ice breaker or warm up for that class meeting. Each time we do the reflection sharing, I ask students to pair with someone they do not know, which results in building and developing the informal social networks that can provide important support for learning both inside and outside the classroom.

Remaining with the topic of students as a source of feedback, we shift now from student-to-student feedback to an important autodidactic frame. Students can also be useful sources of feedback to themselves. For example, systematic self evaluation by students can serve as a significant source of information that can be used by students in combination with information from other sources to triangulate their understanding of their work in the course and of themselves as learners.

For example, I use student self evaluation in connection with grading "class participation." Class participation is a phrase that appears in the grading section on many, if not most, college syllabi. Normally, it accounts for a certain percentage of the course grade but has no explicit mechanism for measuring it over the course of the semester. Generally, it functions as a fudge factor which allows us to make summative grade adjustments up or down from the students' recorded work based primarily on our intuition. "I grade holistically," some say. Being a social scientist and having wrestled for over 30 years with the issues of apprehending the lived experience of other human beings, I have little illusion that I can know the degree to which each of thirty students are participating during a class meeting and remember all thirty of those most likely inaccurate phenomenological apprehensions on my part for an entire semester in order to render a valid summation of each student's class participation.

For me, I want a mechanism for accumulating scores for student participation on a class by class basis. I want some regular indication of the degree to which the student did the homework or prepared for class (I require specific reading, writing, and project assignments, and a minimum of two hours of homework per week per credit hour, which means six hours for a three credit course) as well as the degree to which the student was engaged mentally in the activities throughout the class or participated in the class. I make it clear that session participation, or being engaged, does not necessarily mean speaking. Only the students themselves know what they are thinking about—the class, their grocery list, or a party last night. So for me, class participation involves session preparation and session participation. Each class session, students evaluate themselves for each of these sets of work for that particular class. Students give themselves points for the degree to which they did the homework and the degree to which they were engaged mentally. They submit their scores on a slip of paper at the end of each session, which often they also use to provide some brief explanation of their scoring, although I do not require justification.

The mechanism works remarkably well on a number of fronts. It encourages students to reflect each meeting on their learning behavior related to the course and to provide themselves on regular basis feedback on this behavior. Also, this self evaluation functions similarly to the written reflection paper, where the students knowing that they are going to write about what stood out them about the reading read differently and more productively than if they are merely completing an assignment. Knowing that they are going to rate themselves on the degree to which they pay attention in class and are mentally engaged seems to encourage students to participate in class more actively and responsibly than if they are merely fulfilling a requirement to just be there. This self evaluation introduces reflection, accountability, and ethical dimensions to the students' class work. They can choose not to do the homework or not to engage mentally in the class session. However, if they make that choice, then they have either to accept the consequence of fewer than optimal points or they have to lie. I have been amazed at how few students have blatantly lied and abused this self report technique over the 25 years that I have used it. Incidentally, if the students do lie, I confront them and ask them to change their score. For example, if students give themselves full participation points but fall asleep in class or arrive 15 minutes late, I simply bounce their self report back to them, point out the inconsistency, and request that they re-submit. I explain the reasoning behind this self evaluation and how seriously I take it as a part of the instructional process at the first class meeting, and I reinforce its importance frequently throughout the course. The practice has many benefits not the least of which is providing the learner with generative feedback.

Mastery learning programs. Another source of non-teacher instructional feedback (NIF) is the mastery learning program, which is essentially a tutorial through which students progress on their own, using material, receiving feedback from the program itself, and learning as they go. In the relative old days, although "computer assisted instruction" was around, these self-paced programs were usually print-based with the feedback coming from the answers in the back of the book. Of course, now with the dizzying advances in computer hardware and software, these programs routinely come on CD-ROMs or are web-based and may be phenomenally interactive. Some programs do initial assessments of learner knowledge and tailor the tutorial automatically to the particular individual with whom the program is interacting. The programs continue to interact with the learner's performance and individualize ensuing content as that specific student proceeds through the learning unit or units. The highly competitive textbook market presses more and more textbooks to come with these CD-ROM-based or web-based supplements. The key is that the learning programs are not just sources of information. They need to have thoughtful ways for the students to use their understanding of the material and to receive feedback on their performance. Feed-back provided by essentially robots can play a constructive role for student learning. Of course, these robots cannot replace teachers, but they can free up time for teachers to provide more sophisticated and thoughtful feedback to students than merely, for example, checking a student's definition of a basic term right or wrong and supplying the correct definition if necessary.

Some of these programs have tremendous potential both in terms of student learning and helping teachers to avoid overload. For example, basic writing and numeracy skills are fundamental to many subjects across the curriculum. Some professors spend enormous amounts of time explaining how to write a term paper and how to interpret basic graphs, for example. Self-paced learning programs exist for basic English and mathematics which can be used effectively not only for developmental courses (pre-college English and mathematics) but also across the curriculum as supplements to any course that relies on basic writing or mathematical competence. A site license may be purchased for an entire campus, and students may have access to the tutorials both on a CD-ROM which every student receives and on the web. Professors can refer students to particular sections of the English and mathematics programs as they become aware of students learning needs based on the students' performance, thus allowing the programs to provide students with further feedback in lieu of the professors. Also, professors can integrate the programs into their syllabi and at the appropriate place assign the students to go through a particular unit or units in the English or mathematics programs. For example, a psychology professor who is teaching an introductory course may assign the unit on graphs from the mathematics program along with a reading which the professor knows will require the students to be facile with interpreting graphs. Or a history professor who is teaching a lower division, general education course might assign students to complete the unit on paper organization in the English program just prior to the assignment of the student submitting their first paper. In the fictional future of "Star Wars," Luke Skywalker certainly benefited from the instructional feedback of robots. Nowadays, our students can, too.

Outside experts. Outside experts can also serve as sources of valuable instructional feedback for student that does not come from the professor. We can create a variety of opportunities for students to interact with these subject experts who are not us. Just like the supplemental learning programs, optimally, we want to create or encourage circumstances in which these experts are not only sources of information for the students—of content—but also, sources of feedback on student learning.

Using outside experts is certainly nothing new. Teachers have been employing guest experts, panels of experts, field interviewing of experts, and the like for a long time. Now with email, creating contacts between students and experts has more options. If we are using a course management system (such as Blackboard or WebCT) to enhance our course, we can easily add the email address of an expert to our course discussion board or chat room (with the expert's permission). Say we know personally the author of one of our texts or an article that we have assigned. Using the discussion board tool, students can interact with the author of the work that they are reading in a medium that is convenient for the expert because the interaction is asynchronous and has boundaries (say the teacher arranges with experts to take them off after a specific length of time, perhaps two days, for instance).

The feature that I am promoting here that may be new for some teachers is the notion of using outside experts not just for new content but also for feedback on student learning. This feedback dimension needs to be structured into the assignment by us and is an explicit use of a NIF (non-teacher instructional feedback). For example, formerly, I gave informational interview assignments where students would interview human service professionals who were doing the work to which the students aspired. With a slight adjustment to this assignment—requiring the students to present to the expert the student's view on some pertinent professional issue and then eliciting the expert's feedback about the student's position—the expert became a non-teacher instructional feedback source rather than merely an informational source. With a similar adjustment to all of students' interactions with outside experts, we enrich the instructional feedback that students receive considerably without adding a task to our load. Win-win solutions of this type—maintaining or increasing the instructional feedback for students while also easing the time demands on teachers—is precisely the kind of applications for which we are looking in each of these six chapters (2-7) on "making time."

Research data bases. Finally, research data bases can function as NIFs. Students can be required to take their understanding of a topic to the literature (which can be easily searched electronically) to obtain feedback on the validity of their understanding vis-à-vis the latest theory and research. Essentially, the same skills that a student would use to look up books in the library can be used to search the latest findings in the scholarly literature. If students know how to find a book in the library—and if they don't, "Houston, we have a problem"—then they can search a data base of scholarly publications.

ERIC is an example of one of these data bases with which many professors are familiar. Most disciplines have some similar web-accessible repositories to which we can direct students. ERIC, like most of these scholarly data bases, can provide article abstracts that are sufficiently high quality and complete as to make it possible to get the essential findings of the research without necessarily obtaining the entire article. In a relatively short period of time, students can assemble the abstracts from the latest published work on a particular subject.

Incidentally, if you not familiar with ERIC and you are teaching—regardless of subject—I strongly encourage you to add it to the circle of sites that you frequent. Whenever you have college teacher questions—for example, "I wonder if there is any research on motivating students, or having students evaluate each other's work, or running online discussions, or integrating service learning, or fill in the blank?"—this data base provides you with a fairly up-to-date and complete answer. Not all published work on college teaching and learning is in the data base, but the lion's share is.

As with interviewing experts, we need to structure the assignment in such a way that students actually get feedback on their understanding of the material from the data base and not merely use it to get more information, although that also will be an outcome of students interacting with the data base. For example, we could assign students to develop a hypothesis about a particular topic based on their understanding of the reading and class presentations, and then send them to the research data base to identify specific studies that support and deny their hypothesis, with the requirement to explain whether or not they have revised their hypothesis (or understanding) regarding the topic and why.

The search engine Google (http://www.google.com) has now, for better or worse, entered the domain of popular speech as a verb. For example, in a recent popular film, I heard the working-class, single mom tell her 10 year old son, "Google it at school," and the son knew exactly what to do. So "google" has become in popular parlance the equivalent to my father's imperative to me when I was 10 years old, "Go look it up," which sent me down the hall to the encyclopedia. Our students can certainly search these data bases.

In looking for ways for teachers to share responsibility with other agents in the learning environment, this chapter has focused on examples related to providing students with feedback. I have done so because of the critical role that feedback plays in the students' learning processes and because providing high quality feedback is potentially so time consuming for the teacher. Providing feedback probably receives less attention from most teachers than providing basic content, which is another reason to emphasize it here. Most of us need more help with generating feedback than content. I should note that with regard to shifting the responsibility to provide course content from the teacher to other agents, all of the NIFs that we have just discussed could be used as sources of content as well as feedback. In addition, before closing this chapter, I would like to discuss briefly three other examples of shifting the responsibility from the teacher to other agents that you might find conducive to student learning as well as time liberating for teachers.

Require Students To Download and Print Course Materials

I think that students should take more responsibility than many of us require of them for acquiring basic course materials, such as the course syllabus and handouts. We require them to go to the bookstore and buy the textbook; we can also require that they obtain other course materials. For example, by enhancing our courses with Blackboard or WebCT, we acquire the ability to make easily available for all students basic course materials 24 X 7. If we place the syllabus, handouts, and supplementary information on the web-enhanced course site, then we can legitimately shift the responsibility to students to download and print those materials. We may distribute the syllabus the first day of the course, but after that, if the student loses it, the student needs to go to the course site and download and print the syllabus themselves. We can legitimately assign students to download and print handouts for a class session. If they neglect to do it, then a negative consequence should ensue, such as having preparation points deducted. If students lose handouts or miss a class session, they have the responsibility to obtain the material from the course website, something which they can do easily any time of day or night.

We do the students no favor by enabling—permitting, rewarding, and reinforcing—dependent or even irresponsible behavior. I am a longtime, proponent and practitioner of learner-centered teaching. However, learner-centered pedagogy does not mean always making things as easy as possible for students any more than it means necessarily using experiential learning techniques and small group breakouts. Learner-centered teaching has a virtually infinite number of manifestations. Most fundamentally, being learner-centered means approaching teaching phenomenologically from the point of view of the learners. When I look at what students learn when they are asked to take responsibility for parts of the course in ways that are well within their capacity to do so, I see students learning some valuable lessons that relate to their ability to be a responsible member of a group and to their development as self-directed learners. Requiring students to take responsibility for acquiring these materials (similar to buying the textbook) is another example of a win-win solution: student development is promoted simultaneously with freeing the teacher from time consuming tasks.

Require Students To Monitor Their Own Completion of Course Assignments

I cannot calculate how many hours I have spent, at the request of students, looking up how many reflection papers they have submitted and determining whether or not they owe me some, but it is a lot. Checking basic course records is not the most productive use of a teacher's time. Now, it is also unnecessary. Course management systems allow us to make available to students our records of their submitted work. Students can access their own—and only their own—grade book for our courses via the Internet whenever they want. We need to make it the responsibility of students to monitor their completion of course assignments by checking our web-enhanced course site. The teacher does not have to spend time looking up what can sometimes feel like endless questions about whether or not students have turned in all of their work. Students can do that themselves online.

Require Students To Prepare Their Own Study Guides

I have arrived at this heretical position—to cease the practice of providing students with study guides—because it has now become clear to me that on many of our campuses the professor's study guide may constitute the only course reading that some students do. In my travels, a stunningly high number of professors have reported that their students routinely ask them whether or not they need to buy the required textbook. Apparently, across the country, students ask their dumbfounded teachers, "Do I have to buy the textbook." The meaning of the word "required" has eroded for many students to become similar to that of "suggested." Some teachers have succumbed, with the most compassionate and honorable of intentions, to making "Cliff Notes" (called study guides) for their courses, which the students read in lieu of texts, handouts, and class notes. On some campuses, if a teacher does not provide these study guides, students complain bitterly and assert that ALL of their other teachers do it, which is often interpreted by teachers—and rightly so—as students extorting study guides for good course evaluations (which of course can play a prominent role in promotion, tenure, and merit decisions). I may be old fashioned (notwithstanding my earring), but I think that "required work" should actually be required. We need to make it the responsibility of students to experience all of the required course material, take notes, and prepare their own study guides (perhaps as a group project). Again, I believe this measure to be an example of a win-win teaching practice: students learn more while the teacher frees up time for other critical teacher work.

In the next chapter, we turn to creating a productive time and space for each aspect of our teacher work.

CHAPTER 5

FOR EVERY ASPECT OF YOUR TEACHING, FIND A TIME AND PLACE BEFITTING IT

Related overload adaptation: "...reception is blocked off prior to entrance into a system..." (Milgram, 1970, p. 1462)

"There is a time for everything, and a season for every activity under heaven" (Ecclesiastes, 3:1). And a place, I would add. For every aspect of our teaching we need to find a time and place befitting it. Otherwise, we fight the place and feel even more overloaded. Sometimes places need shaping, and we need to be able to create the kind of place that we need by blocking access to us in that physical locale.

Some teaching activities require privacy. Actually, most teaching activities require privacy or our ability to create boundaries and to prevent interruption. When we meet as a group, for example, we need to have a classroom environment in which we can have undisturbed focus on the learning activities. When we meet students individually for advising, we need to be able to concentrate on each student without distraction. When we prepare a presentation for class, we need to be able to be to think and create without intrusion. When we review student work and provide feedback, similarly, we benefit from being able to concentrate on the work before us without diversion.

When we want privacy, we may say, "I need some space." This phrase means time and separation; it means isolation from demands from others; it means having boundaries that become, for a time, impermeable. In Chapter 3, we focused on defining the amount of time that we want to assign to the major areas of our work as professors, including teaching. This chapter explores creating the appropriate places that go with those times. Having time to create class activities or to provide students with feedback on their work is useless (or a waste of time) if we cannot protect those times from interruption and diversion because, quite simply, the allotted time is not being used for the intended purpose. We need to be able to set boundaries and when appropriate close off access to us.

In 1968, when I was a first-year college student, I went to my academic adviser's office for our initial meeting. He was a full professor and plenty busy. However, when I arrived, he closed the door and gave me his undivided attention. The telephone rang as we were talking. This event was occurring a decade or more before answering machines were standard issue for university professors. In those days, if you did not answer the telephone, the call and whatever information might be conveyed to you were lost, as far as you knew. My adviser held his gaze on me as the telephone rang relentlessly. Being 18 years old, my focus was considerably less disciplined than his, and I finally erupted, "Aren't you going to answer that?" To which he replied, "You took the trouble to come here to see me. You come first." Then, on cue, as if by magic, the telephone stopped, and we went on. I learned so much in that first meeting with that professor: that I mattered to this successful person; that large principles which involved making the world a better place could be expressed meaningfully in small, everyday acts; that a successful adult could refuse to go along with convention; and that I could—just maybe—also make choices as this professor did to live intentionally in correspondence with my values. Obviously, I remember the event vividly to this day, some thirty-five years later.

These themes—intentionality, values, boundary management—continue in this chapter as we explore ways in our teaching lives to create places for our work with firm boundaries and to control—even block—the information flow across those boundaries when necessary.

Teaching Applications

Identify the Major Activities of Your Teaching Work

What are you intending to do as a teacher? What major activities does your teaching work comprise for you? For what are you holding yourself accountable? Recall the exercise and your responses from Chapter 3. Let's say that you identify the facets of your teaching work as follows:

- Course planning and preparation
- Classroom facilitation
- Evaluating student work and giving feedback
- Advising
- Keeping up with the scholarship of your course subjects as well as that of teaching and learning

Allocate Time to Each Type of Work

Continuing on with our example from Chapter 3, let's say that we have determined that in order to live a balanced, healthy life, we will give on average 50 hours per week to our professorial work. Furthermore, we allocate on average 50% that time—or 25 hours per week—to our teaching, which in a four-course load we distribute as follows each week:

- Course planning and preparation (1 hour X 4 courses) = 4 hours
- Classroom facilitation (3 hours X 4 courses) = 12 hours
- Evaluating student work and giving feedback (1 hour X 4 courses) = 4 hours
- Advising (office hours) = 4 hours
- Keeping up with the scholarship of your course subjects as well as that of teaching and learning = 1 hour

Remember that this set of activities and times is merely an example and that yours may look completely different depending on how you define your teaching work, how much time you give to your teaching, and how you choose to allocate that time among your various teaching activities.

Create a Place Befitting Each Activity

We need to create not only time for our work but also place. We need to seek congruence between the desired behavior and the characteristics of the environment in which we attempt to perform that behavior. Otherwise, we fight our environment and divert our energy from its desired use. This "fighting" with our environment contributes significantly to our feeling overloaded. So for each of your teaching activities try to identify places in which those activities will occur that support rather than hinder each one of them.

For example, I cannot think, reflect, and create well where I can hear specific conversations or lyrics. In environments with televisions, radios, CD players, or real people conversing in a way that I can hear their words cause me to spend most of my psychic resources trying to block out what is being said rather than giving those resources to my thinking.

Also, a strong base line in amplified music challenges me mightily. The dreaded subwoofer, which in an automobile sound system is fully capable of penetrating interior offices on the fifth floor of downtown office buildings, is one of my greatest environmental nemeses. I know this fact because I had such an office at Portland State University and suffered many such unwanted penetrations. I found myself continually and unavoidably amazed and eventually irritated by the thought that five stories below me on the other side of thick walls of steel, brick, and mortar inside an enclosed car which sat at a traffic light in thick downtown traffic muffled by a steady Oregon winter rain and wet traffic white noise was a human being who by choice was listening to music played so loudly and subwoofed so profoundly that it vibrated my lung membranes all this distance and insulation away. Instead of thinking my thoughts related to my chosen intellectual task, I puzzled over questions such as: Is it painful to be in the car? How much hearing loss is that person suffering at this very moment? Does listening to loud music make you need to have the music louder and louder to get the same effect as you grow deafer and deafer? Is this person the unfortunate victim of a spinning class where everyone pedals stationery bicycles while ear splitting music plays and a leader barks hugely amplified instructions? Is this person wearing ear plugs for protection? If this person is wearing earplugs, what's the point of having the music so loud? Is the physical sensation of having your lungs vibrate actually the point? Is that person aware of the kind of sonic pollution that they are creating? Does anyone like this? Am I really out of it? Am I too sensitive for modern, much less postmodern, life? Is legislation being written for this sonic pollution problem? Isn't damage done by this subwoofing tantamount to damage done by second hand smoke? And on and on.

I could successfully carve out two hours to read some new material and create a new presentation and activity for one of my courses. However, if I tried to do it in my noisy office, the time was often not just wasted but counter-productive. I came out of the time feeling stressed from fighting my environment and more overloaded than when I went into the time because I had not gotten done what I needed to get done. So for this reason, among others, I did not try to do serious thinking, reflecting, and creating in that office. Of course, we are all distracted by different things, and your examples will probably be different than mine.

Our experience of place relates to the physical and social characteristics of the setting but also to our own psychological makeup which we bring to that setting. We may each of us experience the same environment quite differently. In assigning places as well as times to our various teaching activities, we need to try to be as aware as possible of how we actually experience various settings as opposed to how we think that we should experience them.

Be Able To Block Access To You

As mentioned previously, most of our teaching work benefits from something that could be called privacy or an uninterrupted focus on a particular activity, such as course preparation, classroom interaction, student advising, evaluation of student work, or course-related scholarship. So for most of our teaching work, we benefit from having psycho-social-physical boundaries for that work that we can make impermeable when necessary.

Even so, I focus here on the parts of our teaching work

that require our thinking, reflecting, or creating—activities such as are involved with our course preparation and planning, evaluating student work and grading, and scholarship related to our courses and to teaching and learning. This kind of contemplative or creative work is probably the most vulnerable to interference and requires our most serious attention in designating and shaping places—as well as times—for it to happen. Of all the types of teaching work, I believe that thinking is probably the one that gets violated the most as we become overloaded and whose absence, in a kind of negative spiral, has the greatest potential to make us feel overloaded.

Mortimer Adler observed, "You have to allow a certain amount of time in which you are doing nothing in order to have things occur to you, to let your mind think." In graduate school, I was asked to house sit for one of my department's senior professors, who was widely regarded as one of the most creative minds in our discipline and who when he died was honored not only by the major scholarly societies but also by the New York state legislature. In preparation, the designated, graduate student house sitter spent the night with this professor and his wife getting to know the house, one's duties, and the couple better, which I did. Early the next morning, after an enjoyable evening of conversation and house sitting orientation, about 5 AM, I heard the professor in the living room, where I discovered him, sitting in his bathrobe with his familiar pad and ballpoint pen, staring off at nothing in particular but clearly focused on something in his mind. He seemed oblivious to my presence, and I left it that way. Later over breakfast, he explained to me that he had a daily ritual of rising early and free-thinking, with his pad there to help him to collect and play with ideas that might occur to him. No matter what came up each day and no matter how distracted he might become, he gave protected time and space to his intellectual creativity. It was his discipline. In the time slot that I was dedicating to pushups, he thought.

Some of us easily create the time and space for thinking. However, in order to do better at creating that protected time and space, many of us need ideas and support, which may include simply feeling a sense of permission to do what we know that we need to do. The following four ideas and encouragements may help. If they do not work for you, press yourself to discern what does.

Leave the office. Many of us have trouble closing our office doors when it is time to prevent access. Even if we do close our doors, and even if we do put up signs on these closed doors with our own clever little ways of saying in no uncertain terms "DO NOT DISTURB," the knocks come anyway. That's fine because I strongly recommend leaving the office when we want to do contemplative or creative work. Why fight it?

New faculty are sometimes flabbergasted to learn that faculty offices are normally social spaces, not quiet, reflective spaces over which occupants have a great deal of control. Offices are often useful for advising students, conferring with colleagues, electronic correspondence, and so forth. However, when we are in our offices, we are highly vulnerable to interruption, derailment, and distraction, from drop-in students, faculty, and staff.

Some of us share offices, which compounds the problem of blocking access exponentially. Recently, I was speaking with a professor whose office consisted of partitioned space in a former classroom that was shared with two colleagues. The professor described coolly the challenges of trying to be creative amidst a background of radio programming and near constant collegial, and not-so-collegial, conversation. My admiration for the professor's relative calm grew with my horror at this description of a work environment which for me, with my needs, was on the order of Dante's Inferno.

College or disciplinary cultures may war against our leaving our offices. For example, I earned my doctorate in a liberal arts discipline (cultural geography, Maxwell School, Syracuse University, 1978) but have held tenure and the rank of full professor in professional schools at three universities (Colleges of Education at Portland State University, University of Nevada—Las Vegas, and Eastern Kentucky University). (My story is a long one which fascinates me but probably no one else; so I will spare you the details.) I was socialized in a research-oriented social science doctoral program and my work experience was in higher education not K-12 schools. When I first joined the education faculty, I noticed immediately that many of my colleagues who had worked in public schools and who were preparing students to work in public schools tended to be around the office during what were essentially the same hours as those of a public school professional. Many of my faculty colleagues worked in their offices just as public school teachers, administrators, and counselors did, unless they were in the field visiting schools. In this respect, the college had a school culture. "Being around" was normative for professors in this culture. Notwithstanding the fact that some of us taught between the hours of 4 PM and 9:20 PM, the dean, associate dean, and committee chairs would still frequently call early morning meetings and would drop by during the day expecting to find you in your office if not the classroom. Needless to say, they did not find me.

Leaving the office may be necessary to block access; however, it may not be as easy as it sounds. Actually, I have been surprised at how radical this measure is in some contexts. In some departments, professors' absence from their offices except for office hours is a part of the unwritten faculty creed, but in others, it constitutes heresy. In my case, I needed to negotiate with myself, my dean, my chair, my colleagues, and my students—i.e., I needed to negotiate with self and significant others—to create support for my doing some of my work outside of my office where it made more sense for me to do it. You may have to do this as well. Our colleagues and our students usually want access to us, which may evoke strong, sometimes subtle, sometimes blatant, resistance to our being out of the office. Also, not only do we respond to this social pressure to stay in the office, we ourselves may be another source of the pressure. We may carry within us beliefs, values, and attitudes that make leaving the office not feel right or safe, even when trying to do certain work there drives us crazy. Nonetheless, when it makes sense, we need to be able to work some place besides our offices.

Work at home if you can. Some of us have great work environments in our homes. Some of us do not, thanks to two-year-olds, cramped quarters, intrusive friends and family, loud neighbors, barking dogs, and the like. Some of us, even if we have wonderful work environments at home, cannot work there well because we end up just as distracted from ambient domestic demands as we are at the office. For example, a colleague told me recently that when she was writing her last book her house was never so clean, in spite of the fact that she hated cleaning the house. Some of us work at home just fine without succumbing to the demands of a lawn that needs mowing. If we do, we need to try to take advantage of that productive home work environment and do what we can to protect ourselves from intrusions there. We should not put our home telephone number on our syllabi. If we cannot resist the email signal on our home computer (that little tune that signifies arrival of an email message) or the telephone ring, we need to turn them off or get away from them. Often, our home may offer us more control over our environment than other settings, and if it does, we should use it intentionally when we need to do work that requires us to block access to ourselves.

Know your campus options. Our campuses may offer us places to work in which we can be relatively immune to interruption. We need to scan our campus environments with this objective in mind and catalog these good working environments. We should have them ready to go when we need them, either on a spur of the moment or a regular basis. For example, some campus libraries have carrels available for faculty. We may be able to set up a protected thinking and writing environment just a short walk from our office, which we can use on a regular basis and can schedule into our daily and weekly time/space plan. Usually, we need to be assigned these spaces by the library, and we may need to put our name on a waiting list first. If so, we need to get in line now and not put it off. Also, regarding university libraries, I have found that most of them have secluded places in the stacks, depending on the time of day, which I can use for contemplative work on a fairly dependable basis. Other opportunities may be found in unexpected spaces for which you just need to keep your eyes peeled. For example, the faculty development center that I direct sits in a wonderful 1930s art deco building which also contains a private fac-

ulty lounge, a magnificent sitting room, and a variety of confer-
ence rooms, all of which are rarely used. When my office is too
noisy for some contemplative work that I need to do, I just move to
one of these spaces. Settings that allow us to block access to ourselves may be all around us on our campuses, if we just look for
them.

<u>Know your community options</u>. We can expand this envi-
ronmental scan from merely our campuses to include our communities in order to identify as many places as possible where we can
work and feel relatively safe from intrusion. These places can be
anywhere depending on our idiosyncratic abilities to work in them.
I like to do work such as preparing presentations, reading papers,
scholarly reading and writing in quiet places, which is why I call
these activities "quiet work." So, for example, community libraries work for me. However, Pulitzer-prize-winning novelist Rich-
ard Russo writes in Starbucks-type coffee shops because he has
the ability to block out the largely anonymous world around him
and go into his head for a couple of hours. When he comes out of
his head, he finds the place comforting in that it reconnects him
with the world but does not place much demand on him emotionally. Two of my current colleagues are prolific co-authors of fictional mysteries, and they generally develop their stories in the
corner booth at the local McDonalds—no interruptions, appropriate to talk, plenty of coffee, narrative inspiration from everyday
life all around them...in short, the place is perfect for them. Whatever works for you, use it.

This chapter has discussed the notion that one way to avoid
overload is to seek a goodness of fit between the demands of what
we need to do and the characteristics of where we do it. As teacher-
scholars, much of what we need to do benefits from being uninterrupted. So we have focused in this chapter on developing places in
which at particular times we can block access to ourselves. Having appropriate places to do our work considerably reduces the
sense of overload that comes from two sources: (a) fighting our
environment (i.e., struggling to do what we need to do even though

the setting is not conducive to that activity), and (b) not getting done what we need to get done because we have had to fight the environment.

The next chapter takes up another issue that relates to establishing boundaries in our teaching lives and managing the flow of information across them. In Chapter 6, rather than trying to block interaction entirely, we explore ways to regulate the intensity of our interactions so that we may invest our high intensity interactions intentionally in correspondence with our goals and values rather than using up our precious energy reacting to brush-fires and bushwhackers.

CHAPTER 6

BE SHORT WITH MANY SO THAT YOU MAY BE LONG WITH A FEW

Related overload adaptation: "...the intensity of inputs is diminished by filtering devices, so that only weak and relatively superficial forms of involvement with others are allowed" (Milgram, 1970, p. 1462).

In the last chapter, we identified ways to block access to us completely: we sought places where we could be safe from interruption. In this chapter, we look for methods to allow information to flow to us across boundaries that we set but in such a way that we exercise considerable control over what is demanded of us by that information, and when. Immediate access to us becomes carefully circumscribed and restricted to specific times and places. Otherwise, access to us is blocked (Chapter 5) or filtered (Chapter 6).

The personal staffs of busy executives often provide this filter. They receive the tsunami of information coming at their bosses and pluck out information that really needs attention. They determine what kind of attention that information requires and in what time frame. The staff members have internalized the values of their bosses and use those value systems as frames of reference to make judgments regarding the relative significance of incoming information.

Most faculty do not have personal staffs. Most of us are lucky if we have a student assistant assigned to us each fall, whom we try to teach what is important to us—usually unsuccessfully—only to have to repeat the generally futile cycle again the next year, if we are fortunate enough to get another student assistant. However, this age is one of technological wonders in which I can be standing on the beach in Malibu, California, at 4 o'clock in the morning listening to a quiet, early surf and about twelve hours later be walking across the threshold of my rural Kentucky home to the smell of supper, forgetting my cell phone in a California hotel along the way and receiving it the next day in Kentucky at noon, safe and sound, as a FedEx parcel, thanks to the folks at the university for whom I had just facilitated a workshop.

In this era of affordable technology, we do not need to be big shots with layers of personal staffs to filter access to us. We can use commonplace robots, such as voicemail, email, fax, and electronic discussion boards, to buffer us from the onslaught of information without losing that information and the possibly critical communication that it may contain.

With all of the electronic contraptions at our disposal, we have a considerable amount of choice in how connected we want to be. To a certain extent, we can choose intentionally, in correspondence with our values, how, when, and to what degree of intensity we interact with others. In order to have time and energy for the interactions that we have chosen to be significant, we often need to limit engagement in less significant interactions, as we ourselves define significance.

Using filtering devices to keep involvement with others superficial does not mean that all of our interactions with others are superficial. Paradoxically, these filtering devices create the opportunity for profound interaction. They support the possibility of powerful relationships with selected students and colleagues that are simply hopeless without sufficient time and energy. If I am feeling like road kill from too much unfiltered access to me, then I am really not able to attend to that student who made an appointment to discuss the impact of a reading on her worldview—a crucially important meeting for her because she needs to tell someone (but especially me, her teacher) how for some reason at this very point in time this particular book has made her see that we are all constructing our worlds, "just making it up," each moment of each day and that the belief system with which she grew up was just one belief system among many perhaps equally valid belief systems and was not, and could never be, the one and only truth at least not in so far as she would ever be able to know the one and only truth as a mere human being. Without preventing immediate access by all of the people who want just a little piece of me, I would not be there for her in any condition to listen nor perhaps even there at all. Preventing access permits access. That is the essence of this chapter.

My adviser in graduate school was an intensely brilliant, somewhat eccentric Englishman who did everything with a pure, blue-flame passion. Whenever in the department, he whooshed around the halls or worked at his desk with laser focus. He urged us to learn from him at the same time that he begrudged our interruption of his own work. He told me once that he wanted to wear a hard hat equipped in front with a traffic light. If the light was green, you could talk to him freely; yellow signified that you should approach at your own risk; and red meant scram. I think that he was serious. Instead of a traffic signal on a hard hat, he used facial expressions, which were probably just as effective. Nobody ever mistook the meaning of his red-light look more than once. Essentially, he used nonverbal cues to filter the intensity of our interaction with him. None of us liked it very much. Who ever enjoys being freeze dried by a look? For this reason, in this chapter, I tend to emphasize using mechanisms other than facial expressions and demeanor to filter involvement.

Teaching Applications

Frame Asynchronous Communication Tools as Your Personal Staff

Asynchronous communication used to be what now we call snail mail (or "mollusk mail" as my poet brother puts it), which usually involved a long time between the sending and the receiving of a communication (say a letter) and then a short time between the receiving and the processing (reading) of it. However, with technological developments in telecommunications, asynchronous communication now usually refers to communication (say an email) that we receive nearly instantaneously and then process in our own sweet time. Essentially, the progression has been from delayed receipt/instantaneous processing to instantaneous receipt/ delayed processing.

Synchronous, real-time, or same-time communication—such as F2F (face-to-face), telephone, IM (instant messaging), and chat room interactions—has become a valuable commodity because of its relative scarcity. (Our information environments are so rich and varied now that the burgeoning number of descriptors that we have for different types of communication reminds me of the Eskimos who have seventeen different words to describe "snow.") The demand for synchronous communication from us is generally far greater than our available supply. High demand + low supply = preciousness. We need to invest our relatively precious synchronous communication intentionally in correspondence with our value systems.

Asynchronous communication has always been a way to modulate the pace and intensity of our interaction with others. In the old days (which were not so long ago, given our current warp-speed rate of change), we could let our mail pile up, if we chose to do so, and open it as we had time. Electronic asynchronous technological tools allow us to do the same.

Because of this ability to shield us from immediate access while also preserving the information communicated to us, asynchronous technological tools such as voicemail, email, fax, and electronic discussion boards can function like our personal staff. We need to learn to use them as such. They may not be as charming as Luke Skywalker's R2D2 or C3PO, but these robots can serve us well nonetheless.

Be Proud of Your Personal Staff

Depending on your attitudes related to technology in general and these technologies in specific, you may need to do make an "attitude adjustment" in order to use asynchronous technologies as your personal staff. I have heard wonderfully sophisticated and enlightened professors declaim passionately, "I hate email," or "I can't stand answering machines." I got so frustrated trying to catch one Luddite colleague and friend on the telephone in real time (incidentally, contemporary Luddites come in as many different varieties as vegetarians and may use telephones but not answering machines) that I told her that I was going to buy her an answering machine, to which she spat back with a wink, "Don't bother; I'll pull the plug." Obviously, some of us may have a bigger attitude adjustment to make than others.

Do Not Provide Immediate Access to You except during "Open Door" Periods

Speaking of attitude adjustments, here is an area of our teaching practice that may also require one. Whenever your telephone rings, do you automatically answer it? When that tune plays on your computer signaling the arrival of an email, do you reflexively check to see who sent it and usually open it? Are you unable to close your office door and not respond to a knock? Does doing any the above produce massive guilt attacks in you?

We need to develop the ability to do all of these boundary setting behaviors guilt free as a matter of routine professional practice. In order to benefit from robots who will take messages for us, we need to let them do their work. This point may sound obvious; however, for many of us, we have great difficulty letting another agent do the task that we are used to doing and which we, deep-down, think that we ought to be doing—such as meeting the needs of whoever reaches out to us for help. Many of us have finally resorted to hiring cleaning persons in order to cope with our impossible schedules and still have a house that does not resemble a gigantic science experiment in mold, mildew, dust, and clutter. If we are accustomed to cleaning the house ourselves, being able to be at home when the cleaning folks are doing their work can be surprisingly difficult. The first thing that you know you are right in there cleaning away yourself, which defeats the purpose of hiring the help and probably annoys them at the same time.

If teaching is facilitating student learning, not merely disseminating knowledge, then it is a helping profession, which is similar to, but different from, other helping professions such counseling, psychotherapy, social work, and ministry. Other helping professions deal explicitly with setting professional norms with regard to boundaries and access. Normally, we call a counselor or a medical doctor and leave a message, then we receive a return call. We do not generally have direct access. College teachers need to develop similar norms as we professionalize the emerging role of learner-centered college teacher.

Doing so does not mean that we prevent immediate access to us, always. We still have office hours; we can still have drop in access during our office hours. In my office hours, I always have specific proportions dedicated to both appointments (75%) and drop ins (25%). We can still have regular periods when we can be reached by telephone, email, instant messaging, or fax. I find it so useful when people with whom I need to speak directly tell me that they are available at a particular telephone number on, say Fridays, from 2 to 5 PM. We can still have an "open door" policy. However, we discipline ourselves to set boundaries for our actual or virtual open door and restrict it to specific times that we define. We exercise this discipline as a professional responsibility to get everything done that we need to get done and still remain sane and mentally present when we are serving students directly.

At the end of faculty development workshops, I always ask participants to share their comments with me anonymously on a sheet that I give them with a question at the top: "What stood out to you?" This simple tool has provided me with invaluable feedback over the last 25 years. After a workshop on avoiding overload, one faculty member wrote that what stood out was, "I don't have to answer my telephone. This will change my life." Sometimes simple is profound.

Teach Your Students Your Communication System

Remember that in order to avoid overload, normally we need to negotiate with ourselves and with others regarding our boundaries the flow of information across them. The previous commentary has focused on our negotiations with ourselves: setting boundaries and using filtering devices without feeling guilty about it. This recommendation involves negotiating with others—specifically, students.

We need to teach students our communication system, just as we do our evaluation system, from the very beginning. "This is how you get an 'A,' and this is how you get in touch with me." We need to encourage students to reach us through asynchronous technologies by positively framing the use of those technologies, and we need to explain why we depend on those technologies. We need to avoid being apologetic about it; email and voicemail just are. I think that the jury is still out regarding the hypothesis that some media are "cool" and others "warm" with regard to encouraging or discouraging richness in human communication. For example, online interaction is preferable to face-to-face interaction for some students who may be shy, easily intimidated by professors, or readily distracted by visual information. Used properly, email and voicemail can be useful tools in facilitating our communication with students, and we need to do what we can to help students to perceive them as such.

We need to set appropriate expectations by telling students when we check our messages and by specifying how long students can expect to wait for a reply. For example, "I check my email and voicemail three times a day during the week, 7:30-8 AM, 12-12:30 PM, and 4:30-5 PM, and you can expect a reply from me within 24 hours of my receipt of your message." We need to be clear.

If we expect students to trust our system, we need to stick with it. Our system is a commitment that we make to students. If we commit to getting back to them within 24 hours, then we need to do it.

Our communication system is likely to be something that we need to explain to many students. Therefore, as an efficiency, we should write it down and put in on our syllabi, which we hand out and post on our course web sites. Perhaps we should also have it on one of the information sheets that we routinely give to new advisees, and which we have posted on our faculty web site. Remember from Chapter 2 that any time we set an "educational policy" which we are going to have to explain repeatedly we should write it down for easy and frequent distribution in hard copy and on our various web sites.

Create a Time and Place to Process Asynchronous Communication

Asynchronous communication tools buffer us from immediate access without losing the information. However, we still need to figure out what to do with all of that information.

First, we need to define specific times and places for processing it. For example, if I use the discussion board of a course management system for assigned student discussions of readings between once-a-week class meetings, then I need to select specific times to process the accumulated discussion and to interact myself.

Also, I need to have a suitable place to do it. If my office is highly vulnerable to interruption, then I need to find some place else which also provides Internet access—say, the library (which may be a wireless environment and let me work anywhere in it), an Internet café, faculty computer lab, or home. Recall that Chapter 5 demonstrated the importance of not only creating specific time periods for our various tasks but also finding places that support accomplishing those tasks rather than interfering with our efforts.

Chapter 3 focused on the importance of having a time budget that was rooted in our values and our conception of a healthy, balanced life. These times for processing the accumulated information that has been filtered by asynchronous technologies needs to be an explicit subcategory of our time allotted for various larger categories such as "teaching and advising," "service," and "research."

Interact Electronically in Correspondence with the Time Available

In Chapter 2, we discussed the need to adjust our interaction rhythm to the number of students with whom we have to interact. If we allocate the same amount of time to teach a small seminar as we do a large class, then we simply have less time available per student, and we need to adjust our interaction accordingly. Similarly, we need to fit the depth and duration of our responses to accumulated email and voicemail to the amount of time that we have available. If we have a lot of email, then we need to give less time to each one in contrast to when we have little email and can afford to give more time to our individual responses. The goal is to stick to the window of time allotted and to avoid letting asynchronous communications pile up. We may occasionally receive sensitive communications that require extra time on our part and tend to push us beyond our processing window. However, this circumstance must be construed by us as the exception, not the rule.

As we see in this chapter, so much of "making time" has to do with maintaining our focus on what it is we are trying to do. In the next chapter, we take up the notion of staying focused on the essential activity of our helping profession—teaching.

CHAPTER 7

STICK TO YOUR KNITTING, REFER TO OTHER HELPERS WHEN POSSIBLE

Related overload adaptation: "...specialized institutions are created to absorb inputs that would otherwise swamp the individual" (Milgram, 1970, p. 1462).

Helping professions encourage their practitioners to make appropriate referrals. Doing so is part of the job. Similarly, college teachers (as helping professionals) need to learn that their work sits within a network of professional helping resources—other experts whose assistance we college teachers can, and should, tap. We may be drawn to teaching because we are caring individuals, but because we are caring individuals does not mean that we need to care for every aspect of the student, personally. Developing this ability to make appropriate referrals is another important part of not only avoiding overload but also professionalizing learner-centered college teaching.

Teaching Applications

Do Not Try to Be a Counselor

When students appear to need counseling, refer them to the counseling center; do not just take it on because you want to be a good and caring teacher. Good teaching generally involves helping students to connect the course material to their own lives. Often, good teaching premeditatively evokes personal material from students and intentionally invites them to work with this material in order to connect the new learning to personal experience in some meaningful way. Because most people are a mixed bag of wonderful and traumatic experiences, exquisite and loony attitudes, and sound and faulty thinking, we should not be surprised when students—being human beings—present to us lives with sometimes major dysfunction in them. Actually, we should probably be surprised if students did not do this. It goes with the turf of good teaching. We almost encourage students to bring forth their problems.

What do we do when these personal problems come forward? It seems to me that the fundamental purpose of counseling is personal problem solving; that of psychotherapy is psychological healing; and that of teaching is facilitating learning. Granted, these three basic activities are interconnected, and their boundaries are blurred. Also, you may feel comfortable using different language to label these basic activities. However, I think that most of us would agree that at the core of each helping profession lies a different fundamental purpose regardless of what specific words that we choose to describe these purposes (for a more complete discussion of the relationship among teaching, counseling, and psychotherapy, see Robertson, 2000a). As teachers, we need to stick to the knitting, focus on facilitating learning, and avoid trying to be a counselor, psychotherapist, social worker, minister, physician, or the like, when students present us with personal problems. What do we do when these problems come forward? We should refer the students to the appropriate helping professional on campus or in the community.

Besides not trying to solve students' life problems inappropriately, what should we also not do when students bring their life problems to us? We should not throw up our hands and say, "That's it for active learning. Enough of this learner-centered teaching! Back to lecture! I want an arm's length from these students. I don't want to hear about their personal problems. I do want to do all of the talking! It's a lot safer."

Consider this passage from May Sarton's *The Small Room* (1961), a fascinating novel about relationships between college teachers and students in the 1950s. Lucy Winter, a new assistant professor, tries an experiment the first day of class and talks to her twelve students about the teachers who made a difference in her life as a way to encourage these young women to think about their own learning process. The first person that Professor Winter acknowledges as one of her great teachers was her father. The class ends, and something unexpected happens: a student responds deeply and authentically to her invitation to become personal about the course, and it freaks out young Dr. Lucy Winter.

> Lucy closed her notebook, got up, and was about to make her escape when she was stopped at the door by the Victorian-looking redhead she had noticed early in the hour. The others eddied round them.
>
> That was very interesting, Miss Winter. Especially about your father."
>
> "Thank you," Lucy said. She did not want to speak to anyone at the moment. "What is your name? I must begin to try to remember names…"
>
> "Pippa Brentwood."
>
> They stood there. Pippa hesitated on the brink of whatever it was she wished to say. She blushed. Tears, to Lucy's horror, sprang to her eyes. "About your father… You see, my father died this summer" (Sarton, 1961, p. 37).

At this point, Lucy Winter wants to change her entire teaching philosophy and run for the hills, which is exactly what she does—bolt from the student that is, not her teaching philosophy.

> After all, Lucy had chosen to speak to them first on a personal level. But this intimacy upset her. She wanted to continue to speak to the class as an entity; her instinct was to shy away. She fumbled with her purse and wondered how on earth to handle this plea for sympathy, for pity, for understanding from a perfect stranger.
>
> "Oh, I'm sorry," she murmured. "That is hard. Are you a Senior?"
>
> "Yes."
>
> They were stranded there in the empty classroom, while the roar of life went on around them.
>
> "Thank you for telling me," Lucy said because she could not summon any other remark that would not bring forth she sensed, a flood of tears. "Well, I'll see you next week," and, abruptly, she fled (pp. 37-38).

As the story unfolds, Lucy hangs in there and learns a great deal about teaching, learning, and the complex and highly dynamic relationship between teachers and students.

Teachers who retreat from learner-centered to teacher-centered instruction, or who never venture into learner-centered instruction in the first place, might be similar to physicians who define themselves as medical scientists in the trenches of treatment who focus on the body only, and usually only on discrete parts of the body, giving only lip service at best to the whole person and the mysteries of individual health. They are the authorities who know the medical knowledge base. They frame the problem, analyze the available data, render a diagnosis, state a remedy, and walk away. The patient is a medical problem to be solved. These physicians are generally not as effective healers as those physicians who know their medical science but who also enter into the reality of their patients and treat them holistically within that person's world. If these physicians enter a person's reality and find what appears to be a major psychological disorder, then they refer the patient to a psychiatrist, psychologist, psychiatric social worker, or the like. They do not try to treat the psychological disorder themselves, and they do not stop entering into patients' realities. The same is true for college teachers. As teaching professors, we can take a defensive position and be simple disseminators of knowledge who dominate course discourse with our own voice and point of view. However, we will not be as effective as facilitators of student learning as those college teachers who encourage students to speak out, who enter the students' worlds, and who help student to make vivid connections between their personal experience and the course material.

Do Not Take on Being a Composition Teacher

Do not take on teaching students to write, unless of course you are a writing teacher. Most colleges and universities have a writing center (or something equivalent) that provides support for students needing help with their writing. Refer students to the writing center if they need it.

At the heart of this recommendation is the recognition of

our need to focus when we are evaluating student work. Of all the things that we could possible notice and evaluate, which ones are pertinent to our task? What is our task? We need to be specific with ourselves and with our students. When we make an assignment, we should be as explicit as possible about what we want and what we will be looking for when we evaluate the students' performance. Then, we need to stick to it. Academics in general and college teachers in specific are a discriminating group. Many of us judge a lot, even though we may pride ourselves on our open-mindedness. Our equanimity may often take the form of being accepting of an idea, perspective, or behavior that we have judged to be inferior, as opposed to an equanimity based on being truly non-judgmental in the first place. With regard to evaluating student work, we need to focus.

Student writing may not be central to our instructional objectives. However, as stewards of higher learning and its certification for our various constituents, we may perceive ourselves as having a responsibility to see to it that all of our students can write at the college level. Personally, I think that this responsibility is framed accurately. So a minimal level of proficiency at writing may be a "line in the sand" for us. This commitment does not mean that we need to add giving individual feedback and instruction to students regarding their writing to our list of responsibilities when we examine student work. We need to make our expectations about writing clear to students; we need to identify the resources available to students; then, we need to make the referral when necessary.

Students with writing deficiencies have an extra burden; however, they are not without resources. We are not one of those resources. Most writing centers encourage students to give their written work to center tutors before that work is submitted to professors so that the tutors can help the students to turn in something that is acceptably written. If the students are unwilling to use this resource or if their need is just too great for this process to work, then they may need developmental English courses before they enter the regular college curriculum. Simply ignoring their writing problem does not do anyone a favor—not the student, not the next teachers along the line, not those concerned with the institution's reputation, no one. However, the professor does not need to be the one who solves the problem. The win-win solution (saving time for the teacher as well as getting the student the appropriate help) is a good referral.

"Writing-across-the-curriculum" (where it means that teachers in all subjects provide composition instruction) is a wonderful idea. However, this ambition can run down a faculty because it does not take into consideration the typically overloading demands on faculty, the exception being the rare situation where a faculty's load comprises a few, small classes and the institutional context values teaching over publication. I may be offending some folks mightily, but I am sticking to the recommendation that, as a rule, faculty should not provide feedback on student writing and that they should refer students to the writing center when the faculty judge it to be appropriate. Remember that if any of my recommendations do not sit well with you, use the offending recommendation as a stimulus to sharpen your focus on your own position on the issue and then to reflect on the validity of that position.

Do Not Attempt to Be the Computer Support Desk

Do not take on providing on-call computer support for students; refer them to the institution's computer help. This recommendation may go down a little easier than the previous one for many of us. While most college teachers feel as if they know something about writing, the same is certainly not true about computer applications. Some of us are computer whizzes; most of us are not.

Notwithstanding a self-perceived tendency to flounder in the murky waters of computer-related glitches, many of us wade right in anyway, when a student asks us for help. We may finally begin using a course management system such as Blackboard or WebCT, only to find that we are spending most of our time simply helping students to get on and around the site as opposed to using the technology as a teaching tool (for example, giving our time to answering simple computer questions instead of moderating the discussion board).

Most colleges and universities have specific help desks for students and for faculty with regard to computer related questions. Usually the hours for these computer support desks are quite generous, sometimes even extending to 24 X 7 availability. We need to post the computer support desk's telephone number, and make the referral. Certainly we should be alert to systemic problems, such as the server going down at a crucial time thereby making the timely completion and submission of an assignment impossible. However, we do not need to solve minor individual problems such as forgetting a password. We can appropriately shift this responsibility to the student and the computer support desk. This solution is again win-win: the teacher saves valuable time, and the student learns to use an institution's resources to meet their needs.

Do Not Think that You Need to Be a Librarian

Do not take on trying to teach students to use the library; the library has paid professionals who do that—reference and instruction librarians. Nowadays, the issue is no longer simply making sure that students know how to use the library and its services. The issue is information literacy—knowing how to access and evaluate information. Libraries are no longer merely holdings in buildings, although they certainly do have collections in architectural structures, usually beautiful ones. Librarians are no longer just developers and stewards of collections in buildings, although some certainly perform these duties. Libraries and librarians are about information, writ large. Our students need to know the in's and out's of accessing information and assessing its quality. Recently, I have spent time with reference and instruction librarians, and I have come to learn how unaware most faculty are of this incredible resource. We can take our whole classes to them for instruction in information literacy; they may make "house calls" and come to our classes for presentations; we can make referrals to students to contact them for individualized assistance. This use of reference and instruction librarians produces another win-win solution: we save time, receive better student work, and fulfill our larger responsibilities as teachers in an information age, while the students learn information literacy from student-centered specialists in that topic rather than from overloaded faculty who may be ignorant of the full array of services and issues.

Become Familiar with Pertinent Campus and Community Resources

In the previous sections, I have tried to address some common student problems that college teachers face that lie outside of their primary teaching responsibilities—*viz.*, students' personal problems, poor writing, computer-related troubles, and informational literacy. However, we need to make it a point to become familiar with pertinent campus and community resources for a broad range of other possible problems with which our students may need help. Then, we need to make referrals rather than trying to solve the students' problems ourselves or simply ignoring them. Other campus resources might include a statistics help desk, disabilities resource center, multicultural resource center, international education office, women's resource center, developmental education office, and so forth. Community resources might include churches, various emergency hotlines, as well as a possibly broad array of other county, state, and federal social services.

Have a Current Referral Sheet and Use It

Develop a referral sheet with contact information that you keep handy. Update it as you become aware of support services pertinent to your students and your teaching. Be a collector of resource names and numbers and simply add them to your computer file as you go along. Print up a copy now and then to have available at your desk. You will help more students, better, and save valuable time.

So now we have completed our survey of six principles that can help us to avoid overload in our college teaching:
- *Be able to be efficient in all things:* be able to take less time to do the same things with similar quality.
- *Express your values in how you use your time:* develop a

framework, explicitly based on your values, for making tough choices in how you will spend your time.

- ***Don't hoard responsibility, share it:*** identify ways for other agents in the teaching and learning environment to do what you do with the same or better instructional result.
- ***For every aspect of your teaching, find a time and place befitting it:*** be able to block access to yourself completely when necessary.
- ***Be short with many so that you may be long with a few:*** use devices that buffer you from interruption, while preserving the information communicated, thereby allowing you to respond at a time, pace, and intensity of your choosing.
- ***Stick to your knitting, refer to other helpers when possible:*** learn and use the professional practice of referral, that is, be aware of campus and community resources for common student problems and refer students to those resources when appropriate.

As we leave Part I, "Making Time," try to focus on at least one change that you would like to introduce to your teaching practice or perspective. Part II, "Making Change," deals with how to move from just wanting to make that change to actually making it.

--

PART II

MAKING CHANGE

Right now I'm having amnesia and deja vu at the same time. I think I've forgotten this before.
                                        Steven Wright

As you were reading Part I, you may have been thinking a number of times, "I know that! Why don't I do it?" How many times have we vowed to change something in our teaching practice—add something new or replace a bad habit with a better one—only to fail to follow through? How many times? If you are like most of us, the answer is, "Plenty!" In Part II, we take up one of the reasons why—resistance—and what to do about (these chapters add new material to my earlier book-length discussion of intentional change; see Robertson, 1988).

Significant change seems to pass through three phases in our experience (Bridges, 1980): (a) *endings*, where we come to realize that the old way of doing things does not work anymore; (b) *neutral zone*, a no-person's land where we have no new way, nor an old way, not really any way of doing things, in which we have confidence; and (c) *new beginnings*, where we discern the new way of doing things but still need to integrate it into our perspective and our relationships. Paradoxically, in the beginning, there is the end, and in the end, there is the new beginning. The first step in the change process is realizing that we need to change. We do not let go of our familiar ways easily or gladly. Resistance to change is normal and predictable. We need to understand resistance and how to work through it if we are to accomplish those changes that we want—in this case, if we want to learn to "make time" for our priorities in our teaching lives.

Systems or organized wholes—such as human beings, or more specifically, professors, or even more specifically, you and me—appear to exhibit three sets of forces that affect how they (we) handle change: (a) *entropy*—decay, falling apart, or winding down; (b) *negentropy*—growth, development, or transformation; and (c) *dynamic equilibrium*—maintenance, homeostasis, or just hangin' in there (Bateson, 1979; Boulding, 1956; Laszlo, 1972; von Bertalanffy, 1967; Wiener, 1967). It may be that the most powerful forces are those of dynamic equilibrium, those mechanisms that somehow process complex and continually changing circumstances in us and in our environments in order to preserve our sameness— our survival as we are. Understanding these survival instincts (dynamic equilibrium) and putting their strength in service of our growth objectives (negentropy) is part of the art of successful intentional change (Robertson, 1988). That is what we address in Part II.

Maintaining the "same-ol'-same-ol'" (dynamic equilibrium) is really about resistance to change. Change emerges from a complex interaction of factors in the self and in the environment: in Chapter 8, we look resistance to change in ourselves, and in Chapter 9, resistance in our professional networks.

The scholarship on college teaching has produced some interesting typologies that collect and organize the approaches that professors take to the teaching role (Adelson, 1962; Axelrod, 1973; Baker, Roueche, & Gillett-Karam, 1990; Mann *et al.*, 1970; Pratt & Associates, 1998). A useful subgroup of these typologies organize professors' teaching perspectives into a developmental sequence—that is, a developmental model of the professor-as-teacher (Pratt, 1989; Ralph, 1978; Robertson, 1999b; Sherman *et al.*, 1987). These two chapters add to this developmental literature by addressing the resistance to faculty members' development both in themselves and in their professional environment.

In both chapters, we will not only identify sources of resistance to positive change in our teaching practices and perspectives but also explore ways to work with that resistance. ***If you do not have a specific change in mind that emerged from reading Part I, please select one on which to focus now.***

CHAPTER 8

COMPETING COMMITMENTS AND CHANGE

The constancy and pervasiveness of the operative presence of the self...is the chief reason why we give so little heed to it; it is more intimate and omnipresent in experience than the air we breathe. .... Yet till we understand operations of the self...the ultimate and important consequence is...a matter of accident (Dewey, 1958, pp. 246-247).

$\mathbf{W}$hy don't we change (even when we want to)? That question bedevils many of us. We can "yeah-but" our way around most changes that threaten our dysfunctional, albeit familiar, way of thinking, feeling, and behaving (*yeah-but*: verb, to resist something while appearing to support it, to find fault with something while appearing to support its validity). Change results from interactions among forces in the self and in the environment. In this chapter, we focus on the self—specifically, on resistance to change in the self and how to deal with it. As the philosopher John Dewey points out, unless we understand these pertinent aspects of the self, whether or not the change that we intend actually happens remains "a matter of accident."

Here we apply our attempt to avoid overload in our teaching lives a recently articulated method that shows great potential for revealing to us what we ourselves are doing to interfere with our own commitments to change and what we can do about it (Kegan & Lahey, 2001a, 2001b; Sparks, 2002). As we will soon see, the source of this resistance within us to our development is often some big assumptions that we make without necessarily even knowing it. What we need to accomplish to move through this resistance successfully is some *assumption hunting* and then some *assumption testing*. We begin with a four step process for assumption hunting.

Assumption Hunting

We can come to a deep understanding of our own resistance to change—even change that we say we want—by performing four specific tasks: (a) stating the change commitment (in this case, the commitment to some practice or perspective that will help us to avoid overload in our teaching lives); (b) discerning what we are doing to prevent the change from happening (what we are doing to contribute to our own overload); (c) identifying the competing commitment (figuring out what commitment to ourselves we are serving by overloading ourselves); and (d) discovering the big assumption behind the competing commitment (figuring out why we are so wedded to that commitment to overload ourselves). This discussion explains and illustrates each of these steps in the context of faculty members attempting to make changes that will help them to avoid overload in their teaching. I encourage you to do the work of each step with the idea for avoiding overload on which you have chosen to focus. If you do not have a specific idea yet, Step 1 below will help you to identify one.

Step 1: State the Change Commitment

<u>Commitment task</u>. The first thing to do is to state the desired change as a commitment. Sometimes, the commitment needs to be extracted from a complaint, as Kegan explains,

> ...people wouldn't complain about anything unless they cared about something. Underneath the surface torrent of complaints and cynical humor and eye-rolling, there is a hidden river of passion and commitment which is the reason the complaints even exist (Sparks, 2002, p. 67).

Try responding to the following question: *What sorts of things—if they were to happen more or less frequently in your teaching work— would help you to feel less overloaded?* (adapted from Kegan & Lahey, 2001a, p. 15). *"What commitments or convictions that you hold are actually implied in your...response?* (Kegan & Lahey, 2001a, p. 21). Restate that first response as a commitment, *"I am committed to the value or importance of..."* (Kegan & Lahey, 2001a, p. 21).

<u>Commitment examples</u>. Recall the control/flow paradox discussed in Chapter 1, a paradox that seems central to college teaching (we need to exercise control, AND we need to be able to go with the flow when appropriate). Professors seem to fall anywhere along these two continua of control and flow orientation and therefore manifest a huge variety of control/flow combinations. As examples, we will use two hypothetical professors, one who is highly oriented toward being in control and the other who is highly oriented toward going with the flow.

First, a high control oriented professor who is looking to avoid overload may feel comfortable setting boundaries but wants to become more proficient and effective at it. This professor might respond with the following complaints to the question, what would help you to feel less overloaded in your teaching if it were to happen more (or less) often?

> Students are always making all kinds of special requests. They miss a quiz and want a make up. They miss class, and they want the materials. They don't turn in their work for most of the semester and want me to work with them to get a good grade. It drives me crazy. I wish that they would read the syllabus and follow the instructions. I explain to students what they can expect from me and spell out what our respective responsibilities are—mine and theirs. But they act as if I hadn't said a word and are always whining for extra time, energy, and work from me and special exemption from consequences for them.

Expressed as a commitment, this complaint becomes:

> I am committed to the value or the importance of setting fair but firm boundaries with students and holding students accountable.

Second, a high flow oriented professor who is trying to avoid overload may resist setting boundaries altogether much less managing them. This professor might answer as follows to the question, what would help you to feel less overloaded in your teaching if it were to happen more (or less) often?

> I can't seem to set a plan and stick to it. Everything I do takes longer than I'd planned—preparing classes, presenting material, grading papers, talking with students. I feel as if I'm at the mercy of the moment and never get done what I'd wanted to. I always feel stressed out, behind, late.

Articulated as a commitment, this response becomes:

> I am committed to the value or the importance of exercising more control in my teaching life.

Step 2: Discern What You Are Doing To Prevent the Change from Happening

Interference task. As you go to Step 2, please have a specific commitment in your mind to something that would help you to avoid overload in your teaching life. Now think of that commitment and respond to the following question: *"What are you doing, or not doing* [not someone else or circumstances...what are YOU doing] *that is keeping your commitment from being more fully realized?"* (Kegan & Lahey, 2001a, p. 33).

Our initial response may be denial. "Nothing!" I said the first time that I went through these steps. Upon further reflection, however, I discovered and could articulate particular things that I was doing (or not doing) to interfere with actualizing my commitment to a new way of thinking, feeling, and behaving.

These interferences may be perfectly reasonable things to do, as we will see in a moment. I am not saying that these interferences are manifestations of some kind of subconscious, scurrilous, self-defeating impulse. These interferences typically rest on a foundation of good intent. Normally, they serve to protect us from some horrible fate that we perceive. This self-protection is a noble cause. Notwithstanding the good intent of these interferences, they trip us up as we try to make our desired changes. They are the other player in our drama of dueling commitments—both of which are normally the "good guys."

Interference examples. Our high control oriented professor identifies the following interference:

> I have trouble saying "no" to students' special requests. I cave in almost every time, work things out for them, and then stew about it.

Our high flow oriented professor says,

> I don't stick to my objectives and my plans to achieve them. In the moment, I enjoy letting my thoughts or the class discussion have a life of their own and go where they will. I feel as if I discover things that are of real value which I would never discover if I allow my objectives to foreclose the search. When the foray produces nothing, I feel badly; when we find gold, I feel great.

Step 3: Identify the Competing Commitment

Competing commitment task. Examine what you are doing (or not doing) that hinders your commitment's realization. Try to pinpoint a fear or source of strong emotional discomfort that you associate with NOT interfering in the way that you have just identified. "If I did not do this, then that terrible thing would happen." What is that terrible thing for you? Construe your interference as a form of self-protection—an attempt to prevent that which you fear from happening. Then articulate your interference as a pledge that you hold to keep from happening that which you fear. You are naming a powerful commitment (to protect yourself) which competes with the commitment to change that you identified earlier. This competing commitment is often out of our awareness and sits in balance with our commitment to change. Being rooted in a passionate self-protection or survival instinct, it can have tremendous power in us—it's got juice. This mechanism of the competing commitment serves our dynamic equilibrium (as opposed to our transformation) and functions to resist change within us, despite our conscious intentions. (Adapted from Kegan & Lahey, 2001a, pp. 52-53.)

Competing commitment examples. The high control oriented professor who has trouble saying "no" to students might have these fears:

> I am afraid that if I say "no" to students' special requests they will get mad at me or become disappointed in me. With some students, I am afraid that they might go postal and hurt me or my family.

These fears produce the following competing commitment (competing with the control professor's desire to set firm boundaries with students and hold them accountable):

> I am committed to not being seen as a hard-hearted teacher.

The high flow oriented professor who struggles with saying "no" to flow might express this set of fears:

> I am afraid that if I get too disciplined I will weaken or lose my intuition and that I will block the students from thinking outside the box. I am afraid that I will lose the magic of insight. I am afraid that I will lose who I am.

Preventing these fears events from happening engenders the following commitment (which competes with the flow professor's commitment to exercise more control in the teaching life):

> I am committed to being creative and intuitive and encouraging those traits in my students.

Step 4: Discover the Big Assumption Behind the Competing Commitment

Big assumption task. Big assumptions have some common features. Typically, we are not aware of them, which makes this step of exhuming pertinent big assumptions as difficult as it is important. Big assumptions shape our perception of reality, even though we are not always aware of them. Usually, the big assumptions that underpin our competing commitments involve potentially horrifying consequences. They are attached to syllogisms of catastrophe which follow this form: if I do not behave in a certain way, then something that I fear a great deal will happen. Big assumptions create certainties: if I do not behave in a certain way, then something that I fear will SURELY happen. The syllogisms of catastrophe are beyond question. Big assumptions generally contain an element of truth. However, invariably, that truth is overgeneralized. Big assumptions tend to prevent our perception of evidence that challenges their validity. Finally, groups—such as circles of colleagues, departments, or whole colleges—have big assumptions too. All of these characteristics typify big assumptions for groups as well as for individuals.

If there is a negative in your competing commitment (for example, I'm committed to *not* being seen as a hard-hearted teacher), then remove the negative by modifying the words to form a sentence stem like this: I assume that if I WERE to be seen as a hard-hearted teacher, then.... If there is not a negative in your competing commitment (for instance, I am committed to being creative and intuitive and encouraging those traits in my students), then add negative wording to form a sentence stem such as this: I assume that if I were NOT creative and intuitive and encouraging those traits in my students, then.... After you lay out what you assume would happen, respond to the following question: *How would I feel, then?* (Adapted from Kegan & Lahey, 2001a, p. 72.)

Big assumption examples. Reading backwards through the examples (Steps 4-3-2-1) manifests the inner logic of our resistance to change (the system of thoughts, feelings, and behaviors that maintains our perspectives—through dynamic equilibration—and impedes our changing even when we want to). As these examples of big assumptions are presented, read back in reverse order through the examples of the previous steps so that you can see concretely how something so virtuous—such as attempting to avoid overload—can actually be assumed by us to lead to our own demise and is thereby prevented by us notwithstanding our earnest desire to change.

Consider our control professor who wants to commit to setting firm boundaries and holding students accountable. However, when push comes to shove, this professor can't say "no" to students because of the fear of disappointing or infuriating students. The professor's competing commitment to not be seen as a hard-hearted rests on the following assumptions and feelings:

> I assume that if I were seen by students as hard-hearted that they would retaliate against me on their course evaluations. They would try to get me through these evaluations. I assume that poor student evaluations would create negative gossip and poor teaching documentation in formal reviews of my teaching. I assume that, as a consequence, I would get the reputation of being a bad teacher. I assume that this bad rap would ruin my tenure prospects and irretrievably lower my reputation in my colleagues' eyes, especially among the colleagues whose friendship and esteem I value the most, the good teachers in my department and university. I assume that I would not get tenure and would have to leave the university in disgrace. I assume that I would be unemployable in my chosen profession. How would I feel then? I would feel ashamed and afraid. I would suffer from panic attacks and become dysfunctionally depressed.

Recall the flow professor who wants to commit to gaining more control in the teaching life but whose fear of losing the creative magic of going with the flow engenders a competing commitment to being a creative, intuitive person. The big assumptions and feelings behind this competing commitment are as follows:

> I assume that if I were not a creative, intuitive person, I

would not know how to be, and I would flip out. Also, I assume that I would be miserable trying to do things differently—trying to be more disciplined and controlling of myself and situations. I assume that I would make other people miserable both because I was miserable and because I would be so bad at exercising control. I would do it poorly—be a martinet or something worse. Also, I assume that my worlds be would lesser for not having me to help people to find things they never thought that they could, worlds bereft of serendipity. How would I feel then? I would feel sad and barren. No more serendipity. I would grieve. I would feel awkward and disoriented, not knowing who I am.

Something so apparently positive—such as avoiding overload—leads us through an unconscious but air-tight logic in our minds to terrible consequences. We usually remain unaware of these inner syllogisms with their high-stakes emotionality. Why we do not change is often a mystery to us. The preceding four step process aids us in de-mystifying that resistance. When we become aware of competing commitments and their related big assumptions, we can begin to test those assumptions and perhaps revise those competing commitments. Now we move from assumption hunting to assumption testing which should improve our capacity for self-directed growth in general, as well help us to exercise new ways to avoid overload.

Assumption Testing

Once we have brought our big assumptions more clearly into our awareness, we can act *on* our big assumptions *consciously* rather than acting *from* our big assumptions *naively*. Then we can begin the following four-step process of testing those big assumptions: (a) describing the consequence of holding these big assumptions, (b) scanning for countervailing evidence, (c) discerning the source of these big assumptions, and (d) testing them safely (Kegan & Lahey, 2001a, pp. 81-85; Kegan & Lahey, 2001b, pp. 90-91).

Step 1: Observe Yourself in Relation to Your Big Assumption

Observation task. The first step in this process is simply to take note carefully of what does or does not happen as a result of your big assumption (Kegan & Lahey, 2001a, pp. 81-83; Kegan & Lahey, 2001b, p. 90).

Observation example. For instance, the control professor who assumed that holding the line with students would produce retaliation from them noticed that the inability to say "no" to students was producing a chronic teacher crankiness that made the professor short and sarcastic with students which may have been breeding more ill will in students toward the professor than saying "no" in the first place.

Step 2: Search for Evidence that Undermines Your Big Assumption

Countervailing evidence task. Big assumptions normally lead us to ignore evidence that casts doubt on their validity. Incidentally, this human tendency is apparently so deep-seated that even in communities of the world's leading scientists—who are disciplined to be tough-minded as well as vigilant of other scientists' tough-mindedness—Kuhn noticed that evidence which contradicts prevailing theories is routinely dismissed, often without grounds (Kuhn, 1970). The old saw, "I'll believe it when I see it," probably describes human perception more accurately when expressed in the reverse form, "I'll see it when I believe it." This step asks us not just to open our eyes to evidence that contradicts our big assumption but also to go looking for that countervailing evidence (Kegan & Lahey, 2001a, p. 83; Kegan & Lahey, 2001b, p. 90)

Countervailing evidence example. Consider the flow professor who assumed that changing from a devotion to going with the flow would lead to all kinds of disasters. This professor realized upon reflection that a colleague had followed a personal epiphany a few years back and begun using boundary management techniques to great effect. The use of personal organizers such as day-timers and a greater adherence to class outlines had actually led that colleague to greater creative productivity rather than emotional collapse.

Step 3: Construct a Biography of Your Big Assumption

Big assumption biography task. The work to be done in this step is to identify whence this big assumptions comes (Kegan & Lahey, 2001a, p. 84; Kegan & Lahey, 2001b, p. 90). When did it gain its sway over you? Are there any critical incidents on which it rests? When did you start holding the big assumption, and why?

Big assumption biography example. Take the control professor who assumes student retaliation on course evaluations in response to saying "no" to students. Upon reflection, this professor realizes that this assumption has been a cornerstone of the assumptive world of every academic department in which that professor has worked as a teaching assistant or a professor. Never could the professor remember the assumption being seriously questioned or tested. Pleasing students in order to harvest good course evaluations was simply assumed to be an unspoken part of the game of the promotion, tenure, and merit award system.

Step 4: Conduct Mini-Experiments that Test Your Big Assumption

Mini-experiment task. The final step involves doing things differently and evaluating the results (Kegan & Lahey, 2001a, pp. 84-85; Kegan & Lahey, 2001b, pp. 90-91). The mini-experiment should be *fail-safe* as opposed to *fail-proof* (Robertson, 1988, p. 95). If things do not go as planned (i.e., they "fail"), the consequences should be minimal rather than disastrous.

Mini-experiment example. Say that flow professor designs a class outline with times attached to each section and when the time for a particular section is up, simply moves on. Perhaps that professor enlists the help of a faculty developer (who should adhere to principles of confidentiality). The faculty developer attends the experimental class session (or sessions) in order to make observations and to help the professor to move from section to section at each appointed time. The professor could de-brief with the faculty developer as well as reflect in writing upon the experience of this new way of doing things. Data regarding the students' experience of the change could be collected via a questionnaire or a group interview with the professor absent from the room.

Through the process of these four steps, we gain some control over our big assumptions rather than being controlled by them. Normally, the scales do not fall from our eyes from this process; the outcome is more subtle. For example, after more than a decade of helping people through this assumption testing process, Kegan and Lahey summarize the typical outcome of the individual's work as follows:

> The usual result of such work is not that people slap their foreheads and declare the Big Assumptions entirely false. What more often happens is the sort of thing that is common to adulthood. We add qualifications to our assumptions— riders, amendments, attachments, exceptions. We say, "I still hold my Big Assumption as basically true—but under certain circumstances, with these people, under these conditions, I can suspend my Big Assumption temporarily" (Kegan & Lahey, 2001a, p. 86).

With this work, we lay the foundation for overcoming resistance that is situated within each of us. In the next chapter, we turn to resistance that resides in our environments.

CHAPTER 9
NETWORKS AND CHANGE

*We never educate directly, but indirectly by means of the
environment. Whether we permit chance environments
to do the work, or whether we design environments for
the purpose makes a great difference. And any
environment is a chance environment so far as its
educative influence is concerned unless it has been
deliberately regulated with reference to its educative
effect (Dewey, 1944, p. 19).*

In trying to learn to avoid overload, we are really trying
to educate ourselves to a new way of doing things, and in this regard, as John Dewey advised many years ago, we need to attend to
the educative effects of our environments. Say that we do the hard
work of assumption hunting and testing which we just discussed in
the previous chapter, and as a result, we gain significant understanding and control over our difficulty in saying "no" to students.
With this resistance subdued in ourselves, we resolve to implement some of the practices that we discussed in Chapter 4, which
shift responsibility from us to the students. Specifically, we will
no longer supply syllabi or handouts to students who miss class or
who lose them. Students will be required to download and print
the materials themselves from our course web site. We will take
responsibility to bring the materials to class once, and then, the
students have the responsibility. We have set an appropriate boundary and appropriately shifted the responsibility from us to the students. We are getting the hang of it. Also, if students want to know
what assignments they have not completed or what their grades
are on their work for the semester, they will be need to look it up
themselves on the course web site. No longer will we give our
precious time to these things that it is really in the best interest of
us, our students, and our institutions for the students to do themselves. Then, we go to lunch with some colleagues and listen for

over an hour as they pile up excoriating gossip and criticism regarding other colleagues who do just what we plan to do (or something similar). We sit with sick smiles pasted on our faces as our resolve to change erodes like sand beneath our feet when we stand in the surf with a mighty wave receding around us.

The point here is that change results from the interaction of forces in the self and in the environment. Unless we attend to resistance in both of these domains, the likelihood of successfully changing our teaching practices such that we are better able to avoid overload are relatively small.

In this chapter, we explore a two-part exercise that provides you with a picture, at this point in time, of your *professional* social networks and the degree to which you think that they will support your specific attempts to avoid overload in your teaching. The exercise has a dozen steps—a twelve-step program, if you like. It serves as a useful tool in helping us to shape our social environments such that they help rather than hinder our attempt to structure a healthy teaching life. The first part of the exercise involves mapping our networks; the second part addresses introducing our desired change within those networks.

Networks

The objective of this part of the exercise is to map your relationships with your colleagues as completely as you can. Whether those relationships are pleasurable or painful, supportive or destructive, does not matter. We want to get as complete a picture as possible of the social environments in which you do your work.

When you list someone, use any name or phrase that helps YOU to remember that person even if you cannot remember her or his name (e.g., "bright woman from engineering" or "witty man from early childhood"). You can record your responses in the appropriate section of the figures that are provided as worksheets with each listing request.

Please use this tool to work for you: we are not doing rocket science here. Interpret the following instructions so as to help you to depict your social networks as thoroughly and as accurately as

you live them. Please do not bog down in the details of the instructions. Make them work for you.

Home Department

Step 1: List all of your colleagues in your department (Figure 1). As a rule of thumb, use the unit that administers your evaluation for promotion, tenure, or merit awards. Normally, this will
be the department or unit in which you hold your appointment,
even though your immediate work group may be smaller. For example, if you teach writing as a member of a large composition
program housed in a Department of English and Theater, list all of
the members of the department, not just your program, unless the
program is the group that administers your formal evaluations.

Home Institution

Step 2: List all of the members of work groups at your
institution with whom you feel that you meet frequently, besides
your department (Figure 2). For example, some extra-departmen-
tal work groups with which you meet frequently (however you
define that) might include standing committees, task forces, ad-
ministrative councils, faculty learning communities, faculty meetings of the college as a whole, or the faculty senate. Please do not
include committees which do not meet or the like.

Step 3: List any other colleagues at your institution with
whom you feel you have a relationship (Figure 2). This list would
include colleagues with whom you subjectively judge yourself to
have a relationship (however you define relationship). Personally,
I would not consider myself to have a relationship with those couple
of dozen men and women all of whom worked out at the gym at 6
AM each week day. We sleepily nodded good morning to each
other or vocalized a spare albeit amiable greeting at best, but our
exchanges were limited to that. However, I would say that I had a
relationship with that colleague with whom I shared a beef dinner
once a quarter in order to catch up on each other's live—both of us
generally not consuming much red meat but not being philosophi-
cally opposed to it and loosely reserving our consumption to our
special prime rib ritual at a dark, money green and mahogany ac-

Figure 1. Home department

Sex & #	Person	Matter	Force

Figure 2. Home institution

Sex & #	Person	Matter	Force

cented steak house in Portland, Oregon. This category would include colleagues at our institutions with whom we are friends, even though we do not work together, currently or even ever before.

Outside Professional Communities

Step 4: List all of your colleagues outside of your institution with whom you feel you have a relationship (Figure 3). Possible responses might include members of work groups in your professional associations, colleagues with whom you are working on a scholarly project, community leaders with whom you work regularly on projects related to your professorial life, colleagues with whom you have stayed in touch over the years, or your spouse if you consider her or him a professional colleague.

Sex and Number

Step 5: Beginning with your home department list, then home institution list, and finally outside professional communities list, designate the sex of the person and enumerate the relationships. For women, draw a ○ (circle), and for men, a □ (square). Place the number of the relationship inside the ○ or □.

Mattering

Step 6: For each relationship in general, indicate how much what that person thinks, feels, or does matters to you. You are NOT rating how much you like the person or how close you are emotionally to that person. For example, your arch enemy may matter as much to you as your dearest ally because what she or he thinks, feels, or does affects your life so greatly (say your promotion, tenure, or merit award). Rate each relationship on the degree to which what that person thinks, feels, or does matters to you.

1 = A lot
2 = Some
3 = Little
4 = Nothing

Figure 3. Outside professional communities

Sex & #	Person	Matter	Force

Mapping

Step 7: Sector by sector (department, institution, communities), place each relationship (each numbered ○ and □) on the
network map in the ring that corresponds with how much that relationship matters to you. The closest ring to the center (self) is "1"
(matters a lot to you), and the farthest ring from the center (self) is
"4" (matters nothing to you). Try to place near to one another
people who interact with each other.

Figure 4. Robertson Faculty Network Map

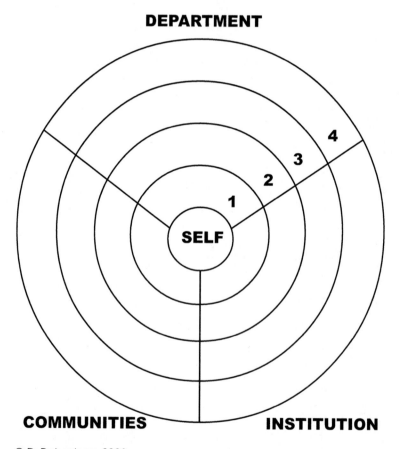

Change

At this point, you have created a visual image of some of your relational networks as a faculty member. Many people find it useful to be able to see these relationships all at once in a glance. How do your critical inner rings appear? Are they crowded? Desolate? How we see ourselves—our actuality and our possibility—while not strictly determined by our social interactions, is strongly influenced by the messages that we perceive or imagine from our worlds (e.g., Goffman, 1959; Mead, 1962; Sullivan, 1953)—our "looking-glass self," as it has been called (Cooley, 1902). If we want to change ourselves intentionally—in this case improving our ability to avoid overload in our teaching—we need to take into consideration the considerable power of our social networks to help or hinder our efforts. Our next set of tasks involves introducing into this relational field that new thing that we want to do in order to reduce the overload in our teaching lives.

Desired Change

Step 8: Identify the desired change(s) in your professional practice. We should all have done this by now—*viz.* focused on some specific change in our teaching practice that should help us to avoid feeling overloaded. The example with which we began this chapter was the shifting of responsibility from ourselves to the students to obtain syllabi and handouts for students who miss class or who lose the materials. In this example, we intended to begin requiring these students to download and print course materials from the course web site. Also, in the example, we planned to implement a policy of requiring students to check their progress in the course on the course web site in lieu of our taking time to look it up, student by student, at each request. Please describe your specific changes now. What do you intend to do differently in your teaching to reduce or eliminate your feeling overloaded?

Force Field Analysis

Step 9: For each relationship in general, indicate whether you think that if the person knew about your desired change in your professional practice that person would support or resist your making it. Return to your lists (Figures 1-3). With the specific change that you intend to make firmly in mind, fill in the "Force" column for each person on the list, using the symbols below:

> +   = Would support your change
> -   = Would resist your change
> +/-   = Would be ambivalent about your change
> [blank] = Would not care one way or the other

Force Field Mapping

Step 10: For each relationship, place the appropriate support or resistance symbol (+, -, +/-, or blank) next to the person's numbered ? or ? on the network map. Simply transfer your ratings from the lists (Figures 1-3) to the map (Figure 4). Essentially, this procedure provides you with a picture of the "force field" around you with regard to the specific change that you want to make.

Observing

Step 11: Examine your map and take note of whatever stands out to you as important. Depending on the magnitude of the change, this step can be quite powerful. I have facilitated this exercise many times with adults returning to college, most of whom were also working and parenting as well as trying to integrate a renewed college career into their already packed lives. Typically, they were experiencing overload in the extreme. In this case, the intended change was going back to school. Some participants would look at their maps and see incredible support in their inner circles. A few looked at their maps and saw nothing but resistance. Sometimes, tears fell.

Change Strategies

Step 12: Determine strategies for increasing the support in your networks and decreasing the resistance, PARTICULARLY IN YOUR INNER CIRCLES. The logic is fairly simple, although I do not want to imply that change is easy. You want to accomplish the following: (a) increase support, and (b) decrease resistance. At least three ways exist to increase support: (a) add supportive relationships (which can be accomplished by adding new relationships or by converting resistors and ambivalents to supporters), (b) increase how much these supportive relationships matter to you (that is, move the relationships toward the inner circles), and (c) increase contact with these existing supporting relationships. Similarly, at least three ways exist to decrease resistance: (a) eliminate resistant relationships (which can be done by truncating a relationship or again by converting resistors and ambivalents to supporters), (b) reduce how much existing resistant relationships matter to you (move them to outer circles on your network map), and (c) decrease contact with existing resistant relationships. Walking through these six possibilities with reference to your attempts to make changes that will help you to avoid overload and to live a saner, more balanced life is worth the effort. Depending on your level of stress, your life may depend on it. Your local faculty development professional may be an important resource for you in this strategizing.

We as individuals are powerful agents in determining our fate. However, so are the environments in which we live. Bucky Fuller was so impressed by the power of environments to shape human experience that he focused his considerable energy, intelligence, and creativity on environmental design as a means of improving the quality of human life:

> [T]o excite individuals' awareness and realization of humanity's higher potentials I seek through comprehensive anticipatory design science...to reform the environment instead of trying to reform humans.... (Fuller, 1973, p. 5).

What will you do so that your social environment works with you rather than against you as you try to learn to avoid overload?

CHAPTER 10
BLESS ITS HEART

I end this short book with arms full of hopes. As we went along through these ideas of ways of "making time" and "making change," I hope that you came upon some ideas worth trying, if not from the text itself then from that which the text stimulated in you.

Also, I hope that you feel a sense of permission to reduce your overload. On their feedback forms, faculty who have participated in my overload workshops have often said that they got some new ideas from the workshop but that the most important thing that they took away with them was a sense of permission to use those ideas as well as the ideas that they already had regarding diminishing their overload. We do not have to choose the pernicious norm of overload. I hope that you feel that sense of choice that you have.

Furthermore, I hope that your paradigm of constructing and using time in your teaching life and of accomplishing change have moved from subject to object in your mind. That is, through heightened awareness, I hope that your approach to time and change have become things on which you can choose to operate intentionally rather than merely something from which you operate, willy-nilly.

I hope that the approach toward overload used in this book—setting and managing boundaries in your teaching life—is useful for you. For my money, deep structural approaches such as this one are more fundamentally effective—that is, tend to eliminate or reduce the root cause of chronic stress—than are stress management approaches which although very important and worth learning tend to teach us how to handle the impacts of stressful circumstances rather than eliminate the circumstances altogether. In particular, I hope that if you consider yourself to be a learner-centered teacher that you see these boundary management skills to be a critical part of your professional development.

Finally, remember that dead horse to which we referred in Chapter 1? That horse represented your approach to avoiding overload. I hope that if you determine that your horse has died you can successfully dismount the darn thing—bless its heart.

REFERENCES

Adelson, J. (1962). The teacher as model. In N. Sanford (Ed.), *The American college: A psychological and social interpretation of the higher learning* (pp. 396-417). New York: John Wiley & Sons.

Aisenberg, N., & Harrington, M. (1988). *Women of academe: Outsiders in the sacred grove.* Amherst, MA: The University of Massachusetts Press.

Axelrod, J. (1973). *The university teacher as artist: Toward an aesthetic of teaching with emphasis on the humanities.* New York: The Free Press.

Baker, G. A., III, Roueche, J. E., & Gillett-Karam, R. (1990). *Teaching as leading: Profiles of excellence in the open-door college.* Washington, DC: The Community College Press/American Association of Community and Junior Colleges.

Baldwin, R. G., & Blackburn, R. T. (1981). The academic career as a developmental process: Implications for higher education. *Journal of Higher Education, 52*(6), 598-614.

Bannerji, H., Carty, L., Dehli, K., Heald, S., & McKenna, K. (1992). *Unsettling relations: The university as a site of feminist struggles.* Boston, MA: South End Press.

Bateson, G. (1979). *Mind and nature: A necessary unity.* Toronto: Bantam Books.

Boice, R. (1992). *The new faculty member: Supporting and fostering professional development.* San Francisco: Jossey-Bass.

Boice, R. (1993a). Early turning points in professorial careers of women and minorities. In J. Gainen & R. Boice (Eds.), *Building a diverse faculty* (pp.71-79). New Directions for Teaching and Learning, No. 53. San Francisco: Jossey-Bass.

Boice, R. (1993b). New faculty involvement for women and minorities. *Research in Higher Education, 34*(3), 291-341.

Boulding, K. E. (1956). *The image: Knowledge in life and society.* Ann Arbor: University of Michigan Press.

Braskamp, L. A., Fowler, D. L., & Ory, J. C. (1984). Faculty development

and achievement: A faculty's view. *Review of Higher Education,*
7(3), 205-222.

Bridges, W. (1980). *Transitions: Making sense of life's changes.* Reading,
MA: Addison-Wesley.

Bronstein, P. (1993). Challenges, rewards, and costs for feminist and
ethnic minority scholars. In J. Gainen & R. Boice (Eds.), *Building a
diverse faculty* (pp.61-70). New Directions for Teaching and
Learning, No. 53. San Francisco: Jossey-Bass.

Bronstein, P., Rothblum, E. D., & Solomon, S. E. (1993). Ivy halls and
glass walls: Barriers to academic careers for women and ethnic
minorities. In J. Gainen & R. Boice (Eds.), *Building a diverse faculty*
(pp.17-31). New Directions for Teaching and Learning, No. 53. San
Francisco: Jossey-Bass.

Brookfield, S. D. (1990). *The skillful teacher: On technique, trust, and
responsiveness in the classroom.* San Francisco: Jossey-Bass.

Brookfield, S. D. (1995). *Becoming a critically reflective teacher.* San
Francisco: Jossey-Bass.

Carty, L. (1992). Black women in academia: A statement from the
periphery. In Bannerji, Carty, Dehli, Heald, & McKenna, *Unsettling
relations: The university as a site of feminist struggles* (pp. 13-44).
Boston: South End Press.

The Chilly Collective (Eds.). (1995). *Breaking anonymity: The chilly
climate for women faculty.* Waterloo, Ontario: Wilfrid Laurier
University Press.

Clark, S. M., & Corcoran, M. (1986). Perspectives on the professional
socialization of women faculty: A case of accumulative disadvantage?
Journal of Higher Education, 57(1), 20-43.

Cooley, C. H. (1902). *Human nature and the social order.* New York:
Scribner's.

Cross, W. T. (1991). Pathway to the professoriate: The American Indian
faculty pipeline. *Journal of American Indian Education, 30*(2), 13-
24.

Deats, S. M., & Lenker, L. T. (Eds.). (1994). *Gender and academe:
Feminist pedagogy and politics.* Lanham, MD: Rowman & Littlefield.

de la Luz Reyes, M., & Halcon, J. (1991). Practices of the academy:

Barriers to access for Chicano academics. In P. G. Altbach & K. Lomotey (Eds.), *The racial crisis in American higher education* (pp.167-186). Albany, NY: State University of New York Press.

Dewey, J. (1944). *Democracy and education: An introduction to the philosophy of education.* New York: The Free Press.

Dewey, J. (1958). *Experience and nature* (2nd ed.). New York: Dover.

Ellsworth, E. (1989). Why doesn't this feel empowering? Working through the repressive myths of critical pedagogy. *Harvard Educational Review, 59*(3), 297-324.

Finkel, D. L., & Arney, W. R. (1995). *Educating for freedom: The paradox of pedagogy.* New Brunswik, NJ: Rutgers University Press.

Fuller, R. B. (1973). What I am trying to do. In V. J. Danilov (Ed.), *The design science of R. Buckminster Fuller* (p. 5). Chicago: Museum of Science and Industry.

Gappa, J. M., & Leslie, D. W. (1993). *The invisible faculty: Improving the status of part-timers in higher education.* San Francisco: Jossey-Bass.

Garza, H. (1993). Second-class academics: Chicano/Latino faculty. In J. Gainen & R. Boice (Eds.), *Building a diverse faculty* (pp.33-41). New Directions for Teaching and Learning, No. 53. San Francisco: Jossey-Bass.

Goffman, E. (1959). *The presentation of self in everyday life.* Garden City, NY: Doubleday.

Hayes, E. R. (1989). Insights from women's experience for teaching and learning. In E. R. Hayes (Ed.), *Effective teaching styles* (pp. 55-66). New Directions for Continuing Education, No. 45. San Francisco: Jossey-Bass.

Heinrich, K. T. (1991). Loving partnerships: Dealing with sexual attraction and power in doctoral advisement relationships. *Journal of Higher Education, 62*(5), 514-538.

Heinrich, K. T. (1995). Doctoral advisement relationships between women: On friendship and betrayal. *Journal of Higher Education, 66*(4), 447-469.

Heinrich, K.T., Rogers, A., Haley, R., & Taylor, A. (1997). Mid-life women doctoral students rediscover "voice" in a community of scholarly caring. *Journal of Professional Nursing, 13*(6), 352-364.

hooks, b. (1989). *TALKING BACK: thinking, feminist, thinking black.* Boston: South End Press.

Jackson, K. W. (1991). Black faculty in academia. In P. G. Atlbach & K. Lomotey (Eds.), *The racial crisis in American higher education* (pp. 135-148). Albany, NY: State University of New York Press.

James, J., & Farmer, R. (Eds.). (1993). *Spirit, space & survival: African American women in (white) academe.* New York: Routledge.

Johnsrud, L. K. (1993). Women and minority faculty experiences: Defining and responding to diverse realities. In J. Gainen & R. Boice (Eds.), *Building a diverse faculty* (pp. 3-16). New Directions for Teaching and Learning, No. 53. San Francisco: Jossey-Bass.

Kegan, R., & Lahey, L. L. (2001a). *How the way we talk can change the way we work: Seven languages for transformation.* San Francisco: Jossey-Bass.

Kegan, R., & Lahey, L. L. (2001b). The real reason people won't change. *Harvard Business Review, 79*(10), 85-92.

Kuhn, T. S. (1970). *The structure of scientific revolutions* (2nd ed.). Chicago: University of Chicago Press.

Laszlo, E. (1972). *Introduction to systems philosophy: Toward a new paradigm of contemporary thought.* New York: Harper Torchbooks.

Lather, P. (1991*). Getting smart: Feminist research and pedagogy with/ in the postmodern*. New York: Routledge.

Lewis, M. G. (1993). *Without a word: Teaching beyond women's silence.* New York: Routledge.

Mann, R. D., *et al.* (1970). *The college classroom: Conflict, change, and learning.* New York: John Wiley & Sons.

McElrath, K. (1992). Gender, career disruption, and academic rewards. *Journal of Higher Education, 63*(3), 269-281.

Mead, G. H. (1962). Mind, self, & society: From the standpoint of a social behaviorist. *Works of George Herbert Mead, Vol. 1* (C. W. Morris, Ed.). Chicago: University of Chicago Press.

Mickelson, R. A., & Oliver, M. L. (1991). Making the short list: Black candidates and the faculty recruitment process. In P. G. Atlbach & K. Lomotey (Eds.), *The racial crisis in American higher education* (pp. 149-166). Albany, NY: State University of New York Press.

Middleton, S. (1993). *Educating feminists: Life histories and pedagogy.* New York: Teachers College Press.

Milgram, S. (1970). The experience of living in cities. *Science, 167*(3924), 1461-1468.

Minahan, J. A. (1993). *Teaching democracy: A professor's journal.* Harrison, NY: Delphinium Books.

Monture-OKanee, P. A. (1995a). Introduction—surviving the contradictions: Personal notes on academia. In The Chilly Collective (Eds.), *Breaking anonymity: The chilly climate for women faculty* (pp. 11-28). Waterloo, Ontario: Wilfrid Laurier University Press.

Monture-OKanee, P. A. (1995b). Ka-Nin-Geh-Heh-Gah-E-Sa-Nonh-Yah-Gah. In The Chilly Collective (Eds.), *Breaking anonymity: The chilly climate for women faculty* (pp. 265-278). Waterloo, Ontario: Wilfrid Laurier University Press.

Murphy, R. J., Jr. (1993). *The calculus of intimacy: A teaching life.* Columbus, OH: Ohio State University Press.

Nakanishi, D. T. (1993). Asian Pacific Americans in higher education. In J. Gainen & R. Boice (Eds.), *Building a diverse faculty* (pp. 51-59). New Directions for Teaching and Learning, No. 53. San Francisco: Jossey-Bass.

Olsen, D. (1991). Gender and racial differences among a research university faculty: Recommendations for promoting diversity. *To Improve the Academy, 10,* 123-139.

Olsen, D., & Sorcinelli, M. D. (1992). The pretenure years: A longitudinal perspective. In M. D. Sorcinelli & A. E. Austin (Eds.), *Developing new and junior faculty* (pp. 15-25). San Francisco: Jossey-Bass.

Padilla, R. V., & Chavez, R. C. (Eds.). (1995). *The leaning ivory tower: Latino professors in American universities.* Albany, NY: State University of New York Press.

Palmer, P. J. (1998). *The courage to teach: Exploring the inner landscape of a teacher's life.* San Francisco: Jossey-Bass.

Pratt, D. D. (1989). Three stages of teacher competence: A developmental perspective. In *Effective teaching styles* (pp. 77-88). New Directions for Continuing Education, No. 43. San Francisco: Jossey-Bass.

Pratt, D. D., & Associates (1998). *Five perspectives on teaching in adult and higher education.* Malabar, FL: Krieger.

Ralph, N. B. (1978). Faculty development: A stage conception. *Improving College and University Teaching, 26*(1), 61-63, 66.

Robertson, D. L. (1988). *Self-directed growth.* Muncie, IN: Accelerated Development.

Robertson, D. L. (1996). Facilitating transformative learning: Attending to the dynamics of the educational helping relationship. *Adult Education Quarterly, 47*(1), 41-53.

Robertson, D. L. (1997). Transformative learning and transition theory: Toward developing the ability to facilitate insight. *Journal on Excellence in College Teaching, 8*(1), 105-125.

Robertson, D. L. (1999a). Unconscious displacements in college teacher and student relationships: Conceptualizing, identifying, and managing transference. *Innovative Higher Education, 23*(3), 151-169.

Robertson, D. L. (1999b). Professors' perspectives on their teaching: A new construct and developmental model. *Innovative Higher Education, 23*(4), 271-294.

Robertson, D. L. (2000a). Enriching the scholarship of teaching: Determining appropriate cross-professional applications among teaching, counseling, and psychotherapy. *Innovative Higher Education, 25*(2), 111-125.

Robertson, D. R. (2000b). Professors in space and time: Four utilities of a new metaphor and developmental model for professors-as-teachers. *Journal on Excellence in College Teaching, 11*(1), 117-132.

Robertson, D. R. (2001). Beyond learner-centeredness: Close encounters of the systemocentric kind. *Journal of Faculty Development, 18*(1), 7-13.

Robertson, D. R. (2001-2002). College teaching as an educational helping relationship. *Toward the Best in the Academy, 13*(1), 1-2.

Robertson, D. R. (2002). Creating and supporting an inclusive scholarship of teaching. *Eastern Scholar, 1*(1), 46-58.

Robertson, D. R. (2003a). Integrity in learner-centered teaching. *To Improve the Academy, 21*, 196-211.

Robertson, D. R. (2003b). *Generative paradox in learner-centered college teaching.* Manuscript submitted for publication.

Robertson, D. R. (2003c). Getting personal about professional development: Why we don't innovate (even when we want to). *Kentucky Journal on Excellence in College Teaching and Learning, 1.*

Ryan, J., & Sackrey, C. (1984). *Strangers in paradise: Academics from the working class.* Boston: South End Press.

Sarton, M. (1961). *The small room.* New York: W. W. Norton.

Sherman, T. M., *et al.* (1987). The quest for excellence in university teaching. *Journal of Higher Education, 48*(1), 66-84.

Shor, I. (1980). *Critical teaching and everyday life.* Boston: South End Press.

Shor, I. (Ed.). (1987). *Freire for the classroom: A sourcebook for liberatory teaching.* Portsmouth, NH: Boynton/Cook.

Shor, I. (1992). *Empowering education: Critical teaching for social change.* Chicago: The University of Chicago Press.

Shor, I., & Freire, P. (1987). *A pedagogy for liberation: Dialogues on transforming education.* South Hadley, MA: Bergin & Garvey.

Sparks, D. (2002). Inner conflicts, inner strengths: Interview with Robert Kegan and Lisa Lahey. *Journal of Staff Development, 23*(3), 66-71.

Sullivan, H. S. (1953). *The interpersonal theory of psychiatry.* New York: Norton.

Tack, M. W., & Patitu, C. L. (1992). *Faculty job satisfaction: Women and minorities in peril.* ASHE-ERIC Higher Education Report No. 4. Washington, DC: The George Washington University, School of Education and Human Development.

Tierney, W. G. (1991). Academic work and institutional culture: Constructing knowledge. *Review of Higher Education, 14*(2), 199-216.

Tompkins, J. (1996). *A life in school: What the teacher learned.* Reading, MA: Addison-Wesley.

Tierney, W. G., & Rhoads, R. A. (1993). Enhancing academic communities for lesbian, gay, and bisexual faculty. In J. Gainen & R. Boice (Eds.), *Building a diverse faculty* (pp. 43-50). New Directions for Teaching and Learning, No. 53. San Francisco: Jossey-Bass.

Tobin, L. (1993). *Writing relationships: What REALLY happens in the composition class.* Portsmouth, NH: Boynton/Cook.

Tokarczyk, M. M., & Fay, E. A. (Eds.). (1993). *Working-class women in the academy: Laborers in the knowledge factory*. Amherst, MA: The University of Massachusetts Press.

Turner, J. L., & Boice, R. (1987). Starting at the beginning: The concerns and needs of new faculty. *To Improve the Academy, 6*, 41-55.

Turner, C. S. V., & Thompson, J. R. (1993). Socializing women doctoral students: Minority and majority experiences. *Review of Higher Education, 16*(3), 257-283.

Two Trees, K. S. (1993a). Mixed blood, new voices. In J. James & R. Farmer (Eds.), *Spirit, space & survival: African American women in (white) academe* (13-22). New York: Routledge.

Two Trees, K. S. (1993b). Visitation workshop. In J. James & R. Farmer (Eds.), *Spirit, space & survival: African American women in (white) academe* (235-236). New York: Routledge.

Von Bertalanffy, L. (1967). *Robots, men and minds: Psychology in the modern world*. New York: George Braziller.

Washington, V., & Harvey, W. (1989). *Affirmative rhetoric, negative action: African-American and Hispanic faculty at predominantly White institutions*. Report No. 2. Washington, DC: School of Education and Human Development, The George Washington University.

Whitt, E. J. (1991) "Hit the ground running": Experiences of new faculty in a school of education. *Review of Higher Education, 14*(2), 177-197.

Wiener, N. (1967). *The human use of human beings: Cybernetics and society*. New York: Avon Books.

Wright, R. A., & Burden, J. A. (Eds.). (1986). *Teaching in the small college: Issues and applications*. Contributions to the Study of Education, No. 17. New York: Greenwood Press.

INDEX